DECIPHERING THE TEXT FOUNDATIONS OF TRAVELLER

and Other Essays

Michael Andre-Driussi

Sirius Fiction

Copyright © 2020 Michael Andre-Driussi

All rights reserved

No part of this book may be reproduced, or stored in a retrieval system, or transmitted in any form or by any means, electronic, mechanical, photocopying, recording, or otherwise, without express written permission of the publisher.

ISBN-13: 978-1-947614-21-5 (paperback)
ISBN-13: 978-1-947614-22-2 (ebook)

CONTENTS

Title Page
Copyright
Introduction
Deciphering the Text Foundations of Traveller ® 1
Deciphering the Texts... Additions, Elaborations 17
Morality Systems in Role-playing Games 21
Languages of the Dying Sun 25
SF Rock: Bowie and Numan 45
SF Heresies #1 & #2 52
Toynbee and SF: Asimov and de Camp 55
SF Heresy #3 66
Wes Anderson and ERB 70
Three Movies Responding to Hitler (1936 to 1941) 73
SF Rock: The Human League 80
Ballard's Debt to Hawthorne 83
Raving on "The Repairer of Reputations" 87
Notes on "The Prophets' Paradise" 94
Spike & Sofia: Their War 99
Alas, Babylon and the Cuban Nukes 106
Notes for Survivors (1975) 109
The Last Defender of Barsoom 112

Review of The Man with the Compound Eyes	115
Raving About the Films of Shane Carruth	118
Stations of the Cross in Stations of the Tide	121
Little Proust on the Prairie	125
Autopsy of SF	131
Bibliography	135
Publishing History	141
Books By This Author	143

INTRODUCTION

Out of the chaos, a pattern begins to form.

Most of these essays, written across twenty-odd years about times and pieces further back, deal with the porous borderlands of science fiction, tracking the flow in both directions. By example, three musical groups who used science fiction with mixed results; a 19th century American literary story that moved a 20th century British avant-garde figure to imitation; the film responses to Adolph Hitler in real time.

There is an investigative side, collectively unearthing a secret history of genre: a popular historian who set the groundwork for galactic empires and altnernate histories; two hidden genre authors whose work shaped a popular role-playing game; the way a paperback thriller nearly came true at the Cuban Missile Crisis; the pandemic apocalypse of a British TV series from 1975 and the Covid-19 situation of 2020.

The two lead dogs for this mush team are "Traveller" and "Dying Sun." I assume that one or the other brought you this far. The team will transport you across strange and alien terrain. I hope they serve you well.

DECIPHERING THE TEXT FOUNDATIONS OF TRAVELLER ®

The book sources for the science fiction game *Traveller* are as obscured as a medieval palimpsest, yet a careful sifting through the evidence reveals the hidden roots, which in turn point to the pathways of genre evolution from 1965 to 2001.

The game *Traveller* (now known as "Classic Traveller" or "CT" for short) was first published by Game Designers' Workshop in 1977. CT provided the new medium of role-playing games with a science fiction setting comparable to the fantasy setting established by *Dungeons & Dragons* three years earlier; CT was not the first sfrpg, but it was the most successful. There can be no doubt the game benefited from the release of *Star Wars* in the same year and the subsequent market boom in science fiction, yet CT was not initially inspired by any science fiction movie or television series; rather, it was driven by written sf. CT sketched out a universe based upon a mixture of elements drawn from a number of science fiction novels, just as D&D had done for fantasy, but where D&D was open about its source texts (naming in the rules book such classics as Tolkien's *Lord of the Rings*, Vance's *The Dying Earth*, and Moorcock's *Elric* books), CT was more cryptic.

There are two good reasons for CT's roots to have been obscured, one legal and the other aesthetic. In the beginning, both TSR (publisher of D&D) and GDW (publisher of CT) were encouraging their customers to "do it yourself" in adapting favorite genre works to their respective games. TSR was so blatant about borrowings that they quickly ran afoul of copyright holders: *Warriors of Mars* (1974) presented Barsoom without license and brought the ire of the Edgar Rice Burroughs estate; *Deities and Demigods* (1980) contained unlicensed material belonging to H. P. Lovecraft and Michael Moorcock, sections later dropped from the second edition (1981). On the aesthetic side, GDW clearly did not want to be bound to reproducing the entirety of an author's universe: they just wanted to take what they considered to be the best bits of a few and make a new, organic whole of it. Call it the "Frankenstein" approach, where a new creature is made from parts taken from anonymous donors.

The look and feel of CT is internally consistent and somewhat generic, yet still rather difficult to match with a precursor. One would expect a science fiction role-playing game set in a galactic empire to look like Asimov's *Foundation* trilogy (1942–50), the granddaddy of all galactic empires, yet CT does not, eschewing Asimov's atomic ashtrays, blasters, the full-metal planet Trantor, and a stardrive of such speed that a trip from the galactic rim to the core can be done in a honeymoon jaunt. Likewise, CT does not look or feel like Frank Herbert's *Dune* (1960s ecology sf), or Larry Niven's "Known Space" (1960s hard sf), or E. E. "Doc" Smith's "Lensman" (1930s space opera). It might seem strange that an sfrpg based on sf texts would somehow miss all the "classics," but the problem is that these classics are mutually exclusive—they cannot blend well together. What the creators of CT were after was science fiction adventure, featuring freelance "adventurers" (with all the connotations of gold hunters, mercenaries, and trail blazers that this term implies) who could live or die in the course of pick-up games. They seem inspired by adventure movies like *The Treasure of the Sierra Madre*, *The Wages of Fear*, and *The Man Who Would Be King*; noir movies like *Yojimbo* and *Kiss Me Deadly*; "heist" movies like *Rififi* and *Le Cercle Rouge*. All of which is the polar opposite of "Star Trek" (where everyone works together for the government; there is a moral code in the "Prime Directive"; nobody important dies).

The amoral (or morally ambiguous) and violent nature of these adventures is attested to by the game's rules:

> *The key to adventure in Traveller is the patron. When a band of adventurers meets an appropriate patron, they have a person who can give them direction in their activities, and who can reward them for success . . . . A patron will, if he decides to hire a band of adventurers, specify a task or deed to be performed, and then finance reasonable expenses for the pursuit of that task. Some tasks may be ordinary in nature, such as hired guards or escorts; other tasks may be for the location and procurement of items of great value. (Book 3, Worlds and Adventures, 25)*

The earliest mini-adventures published in the magazine *The Journal of the Travellers' Aid Society* followed this pattern: "The Ship in the Lake" (1979) describes a sunken treasure in a war zone; "Planetoid P-4638" (1979) is a job of industrial espionage and covert operations; "Salvage on Sharmun" (1980) offers sunken treasure on a proscribed world. The first double-adventures expanded the range somewhat: *Shadows/Annic Nova* (1980) are essentially two "dungeon crawls," one in an alien pyramid complex, the other in a derelict starship; *Across the Bright Face/Mission on Mithril* (1980) are both "wilderness adventures," one on a hot world, the other on an icy planet.

Supplement 6: 76 Patrons (1980), goes much further, providing 60 basic jobs for adventurers. Of these missions, some 10% are morally good (three cases of missing persons, one case each of "find a hidden place," anti-smuggling, and anti-theft) and 20% are neutral (bodyguard, ship work, and "guard a place"). The remaining majority of 70% are criminal activities, including: eight burglaries (five in a Watergate style); four assassinations (two of them political leaders); two cases each of hijacking and kidnapping; and one noteworthy case of global terrorism with a weapon of mass destruction.

This is not to condemn CT but to establish its noir character beyond any shadow of doubt. The universe of CT is definitely not that of *Star Trek*, nor that of *Star Wars*, nor even that of de Camp's "Viagens Interplanetarias" adventure stories. CT is hard-line noir, as exemplified by the logical "sequel" to *76 Patrons* in the form of the full-length adventure *Prison Planet* (1982).

The creators of CT wanted the anarchic, amoral, and violent adventure of fantasy role-playing translated into a science fiction setting. They also wanted a kind of science fiction that used more "hard sf" than even Niven's work. They categorically rejected New Wave sf, which made them allied to the Old Wave, except that GDW wanted a gritty, noir setting (where the Old Wave is characterized as upbeat and moral). This made a lot of sense: the Mystery genre had long since gone noir, and more recently Westerns had followed suit (starting with Sergio Leone's *A Fistful of Dollars* in 1964), so it seemed a safe bet that sf would leave the New Wave and "go noir" in the near future.

In short, GDW wanted a form of science fiction that was as reinvented and redefined as the Western movie had been transformed by the "spaghetti Westerns."

GDW published CT with plenty of DIY ("do it yourself") encouragement for its buyers to make their own settings, since initially they were purchasing a game system with only a vague Imperial background. The contradictory streams of encouraging DIY universes and providing official Third Imperium material began with the first supplement and continued for some time: an appendix in *1001 Characters* (1978) provided a list of heroes "drawn from the pages of science fiction" (43); the fourth supplement, *Citizens of the Imperium* (1979), had a second list of famous sf heroes and villains, and a citation of the sources for both lists. Aside from showing the versatility of the game system in being able to handle famous characters from divergent universes, this was also a possible opportunity to quietly reveal the heretofore hidden sources of CT itself.

Of the fourteen source-text titles, three are single novels and eleven are series. To be fair, the context of the list was "famous sf heroes and villains that could be used in CT," but most of the settings seem like a stretch for the CT milieu (the universal psionics of *The Stars My Destination*; the comedy of the "Stainless Steel Rat" series; and the hospital drama of the "Sector General" series, to name a few). On the following table, "DIY" is the ease of a referee in creating a setting based on the given title, with "5" being the easiest and "1" being the most difficult.

Title	(Notes)	DIY
Barsoom series	(One planet, fantasy feel)	4
Lensman series	(1930's Space Opera)	2
Deathworld Trilogy	(Single planet)	3
Dumarest saga	(Galactic wanderer)	5
Niven's "Known Space"	(Big scale, fast ftl)	4
Panshin's *Starwell*	(Detective comedy)	3
Flandry series	(Working for empire)	3
Demon Princes series	(Detective/Revenge)	3
The Stars My Destination	(Everyone psi teleports)	1
The Stainless Steel Rat	(Thief Comedy)	3
CoDominium series	(FTL jumplines, f. fields)	3
Sector General series	(Space hospital)	1
Retief series	(Diplomat Comedy)	3
The Stars, Like Dust	(Foundation universe)	2

Of all, only one scores a perfect 5: The one title that turns out to be an authentic source of inspiration for CT is E. C. Tubb's "Dumarest" saga.

E. C. Tubb's "Dumarest of Terra" series (1967 onward) portrays its titular hero as a far future Odysseus trying to find his way home across a galaxy that has forgotten Earth completely. Each novel is slim and action-packed: Earl Dumarest arrives penniless at a new planet where he must use his wits and his reflexes, not only to survive but also to make enough money for passage to the next planet. From this series, already 17 books long in 1977, CT got such details as: low passage (a deadly hibernation system); mesh armor; the drugs fast, slow, medical slow, and combat (i.e., two-thirds of the drugs in CT); the weapon "blade"; and perhaps the psionics.

In some cases the original context was warped: in Dumarest's universe, low passage kills one in six human passengers, just as in CT. But it was never meant for human use; it is for animals only (so the high death rate for CT's "frozen watch" of the Imperial Navy is an artifact of this warpage). In Dumarest the wealthy passengers travel "high passage" whereby their subjective time-frames are slowed down by expensive drugs called "quick-time" so that the long voyage between stars goes by more quickly (similar to CT's "Fast" drug, but CT avoided that New Wave "high" passage for aesthetic reasons). Everybody else travels middle passage, that is, in real time.

Low Passage
CT: "Transportation while in cold sleep (suspended animation) is possible at relatively low cost to the passenger. . . . Unfortunately, the low passage system involves some intrinsic dangers to the passenger, and he runs some risk of not surviving the voyage. Throw 5+ for each passenger [i.e., 17 percent death rate]"
Dumarest: "Riding in the bleak cold sections in caskets meant for the transport of livestock, risking the 15 percent death rate for the sake of cheap travel" (*Lallia*, 6).

Mesh Armor
CT: "A jacket or body suit made of natural or synthetic leather and reinforced with a lining of flexible metal mesh, similar to chain mail but lighter and stronger"
Dumarest's signature armor: "Looking down he saw scratches in the gray plastic of his tunic. They were deep enough to reveal the gleam of protective mesh buried in the material" (*Jester*, 13).

Blade (weapon)
CT: "A hybrid knife weapon with a heavy, flat two-edged blade nearly 300 mm [11.75 in.] in length, and a semi-basket handguard. Because of the bulk of the handguard, it is generally carried in a belt scabbard" [note that the CT dagger is 200 mm (8 in.)]
Dumarest's signature weapon: "Transferring it to his left hand he drew the ten-inch knife from his boot, poising it as his eyes searched the darkness" (*Toyman*, 6).

Slow Drug
CT: The user experiences the world as being two times slower than normal. It is used as a combat enhancer through speeded-up reflexes.
Dumarest Slow-time, diluted: "[a diluted dose of] slow-time ... to him, time had slowed so that he could do more in a second than could a normal man" (*Jester*, 9).

Medical Slow Drug
CT: The user experiences the world as being thirty times slower than normal. It is used to promote rapid healing and has sedation built in, but it is often used in conjunction with "Medical drug" to promote further healing.
Dumarest Slow-time: "Beneath the [transparent] covering he could see the flesh almost totally healed. Hormones, he thought, or perhaps even slow-time, the magical chemical which speeded the metabolism so that a man lived a day in a few minutes" (*Jondelle*, 12). Used in conjunction with sedation and intravenous feeding.

Fast Drug
CT: The user experiences the world as being sixty times faster than normal, used as an emergency form of suspended animation.
Dumarest Quick-time: "The magic of quick-time ... slowed his metabolism down so that he lived at one fortieth the normal rate. He, the girl, the others who traveled on High passage" (*Kalin*, 23).

Combat Drug
CT: Provides user with enhanced strength and endurance.
Dumarest Slow-time while conscious: "You said that you knew what you were doing but few have used slow-time in the conscious state" (*Gath*, 163); "He was living at about forty times the normal rate" (*Gath*, 165).

Perhaps more importantly, CT got the name "traveller." In Dumarest's universe this is the term for an adventurer who has no ship of his own and goes from world to world. After the handler has revived Dumarest from the low passage coffin, he asks, "What's it like being a traveler? I mean, what do you get out of it?"

"It's a way of life," said Dumarest. "Some like it, some don't. I do."

"How do you go about it? What do you do between trips?"

"Look around, get a job, build another stake for passage to somewhere else." (The Winds of Gath, Dumarest #1, p. 5)

Nine books later, an observer notes: "A traveler. A man who moved from world to world . . . A wanderer who had seen a hundred worlds" (*Jondelle, Dumarest #10*, p. 6).

On the CT side we find this expressed as: "Looking for work is a constant chore for travellers" (back cover of adventure *Expedition to Zhodane*, 1981).

In his novels, Tubb uses "one-L" traveler, the American spelling of the word. By using the older, British, "two-L" form, GDW deftly evokes an imperial history of far-flung territories: the exotic English-speaking world beyond the American shore: South Africa, India, Singapore, Hong Kong, Australia, etc.

Dumarest of Terra (first 17)

1. *The Winds of Gath* (1967)
2. *Derai* (1968)
3. *Toyman* (1969)
4. *Kalin* (1969)
5. *The Jester at Scar* (1970)
6. *Lallia* (1971)
7. *Technos* (1972)
8. *Veruchia* (1973)
9. *Mayenne* (1973)
10. *Jondelle* (1973)
11. *Zenya* (1974)
12. *Eloise* (1975)
13. *Eye of the Zodiac* (1975)
14. *Jack of Swords* (1976)
15. *Spectrum of a Forgotten Sun* (1976)
16. *Haven of Darkness* (1977)
17. *Prison of Night* (1977)

CT owes a lot to Dumarest: at the detail level there is a ship's locker-worth of equipment; at the thematic level there is the noir, gritty, money-grubbing "traveler" which serves as the symbol of the CT adventurer. One critical thing missing from Dumarest is a galactic empire—for this the creators of CT went to another cryptic source, a text that forms another strong root for CT even though it does not appear in the "heroes and villains" list. This unmentioned elephant in the corner is H. Beam Piper's *Space Viking*.

H. Beam Piper's "Terro-Human" series, a future history of novels and stories covering 30 centuries, collectively had a big influence on CT, but none were so powerful as the novel *Space Viking*. Here was a warrior aristocracy for good and for ill, but not for ridicule (as are the nobles in Asimov's Foundation trilogy). Here were space raiders with no blasters or even lasers, instead using gunpowder weapons and nuclear bombs. (Piper was a gun-nut with quite a personal collection, and his use of gunpowder weapons in an interstellar setting is a good match for CT, where laser pistols were forbidden as "fantasy.")

Space Viking opens on the planet Gram with hero Lord Lucas Trask's bride Elaine being killed at their wedding by the submachine gun-wielding madman Lord Andray Dunnan. Dunnan then steals a starship to escape the Sword-Worlds and Trask sets out to track him down, beginning an interstellar manhunt for revenge, with worlds for plunder along the way. The chase goes on for years, with Trask building up a low-tech planet named Tanith into a Viking base while Dunnan purposefully imitates Hitler in subverting Marduk, a civilized welfare-state planet: only Trask's Space Vikings can save the world.

CT's supplement *The Spinward Marches* (1979) depicted a frontier region of Imperial space, a map for the settings of many published adventures. Near the center of this map lies a group of planets called "the Sword Worlds," each one named after a legendary sword (Excalibur, Gram, etc.)—just as they are in *SV*. But sword names are not copyrighted, so there is no way of proving that these sword worlds are taken from Piper's Sword-Worlds.

Space Viking has very little description of the Sword-Worlds themselves. Piper writes of the planet Gram, "the huge red sun hung in a sky as yellow as a ripe peach" (SV, 1). Before long he compares Gram and Excalibur while thinking of his coming honeymoon with Elaine: "And she would see clear blue skies again, and stars at night. The cloudveil hid the stars from Gram, and Elaine had missed them, since coming home from [college on] Excalibur" (2). Gram's leader, Duke Angus, later calls himself King and exerts control over the other Sword-Worlds.

GDW's planet Gram has this code: "A895957-B." The first "9" describes the planet's atmosphere as "dense and tainted," which is what one would expect for a world with a constant cloud veil and a "yellow" sky. Gram is also the subsector capital, the administrative seat of all the Sword Worlds.

GDW's world Excalibur has the code: "B324755-A." The "2"

means that the atmosphere is "thin and tainted." The stars shine bright on such a planet.

From the micro details of a few planetary settings we move to the macro detail of planetary and interstellar government. Among CT's planetary government types, an elegant Aristotelian spectrum ranging from "Anarchy" to "Religious Dictatorship," there is the curious term "Feudal Technocracy." Curious because such a government type is not known from history, yet this seemingly archaic-futurism is the most desired type of government in the Imperium. Feudal Technocracy seems to come straight out of *SV*, wherein Piper sets forth a libertarian/medievalist model in direct contrast to Asimov's anti-medievalist position.

On the civilized world Marduk, Trask is asked about the government of the Sword-Worlds, the interstellar association he grew up in:

> *"Well, we don't use the word government very much," [Trask] replied. "We talk a lot about authority and sovereignty . . . but government always seems to us like sovereignty interfering in matters that don't concern it. As long as sovereignty maintains a reasonable semblance of good public order and makes the more serious forms of crime fairly hazardous for the criminals, we're satisfied."*
>
> *"But that's just negative. Doesn't the government do anything positive for the people?"*
>
> *He tried to explain the Sword-World feudal system to them. It was hard, he found, to explain something you have taken for granted all your life to somebody who is quite unfamiliar with it.*
>
> *"But the government . . . doesn't do anything for the people!" one of the professors objected. "It leaves all the social services to the whim of the individual lord or baron."*

> *"And the people have no voice at all; why, that's tyranny," an Assemblyman added.*
>
> *He tried to explain that the people had a very distinct and commanding voice, and that barons and lords who wanted to stay alive listened attentively to it. The Assemblyman changed his mind; that wasn't tyranny, it was anarchy. And the professor was still insistent about who performed the social services.*
>
> *"If you mean schools and hospitals and keeping the city clean, the people do that for themselves. The government ... just sees to it that nobody's shooting at them while they're doing it."*
>
> *"That isn't what Professor Pullwell means, Lucas. He means old-age pensions," Prince Bentrik said.* (Space Viking, "Marduk" section III)

The pointed contrast is between a welfare state and the gunpowder-feudalism of the Sword-Worlds. While this feudalism shows some of the checks and balances found in the early United States, some might be tempted to label it "fascism" for the blatant militarism and piracy it displays: yet the text is clear in equating Dunnan with Hitler ("Maybe [Dunnan] was reading about Hitler ... he was planning conquest ... by subversion" (215, Marduk VII)), making the Space Vikings anti-fascist pirates.

Later sfrpg products from GDW continued to exhibit Piper's influence: the source-book *Star Vikings* (1994) being the most obvious case, and the "growler" (an intra-mouth device allowing humans to speak with a species of aliens in *Ranger*, p. 24–5, 1989) being perhaps the most obscure (coming from *Uller Uprising*). The popular Piper novels about "Fuzzies" had no discernable effect on CT, presumably because the fuzzies are too cute for *Traveller*.

TerroHuman series
1st century AE: *Four-Day Planet* (1961)
4th century AE: *Uller Uprising* (1952)
7th century AE: The "Fuzzy" books (1962, 1964, 1984)
9th century AE: *Cosmic Computer* (1963)
1st to 9th c. AE: *Federation* (collected 1981)
16th century AE: *Space Viking* (1963)
16th to 30th c. AE: *Empire* (collected 1981)

The two most important written sf influences on CT are Tubb's "Dumarest of Terra" series and Piper's *Space Viking*. Dumarest answers the needs of adventurers lacking their own ship; *SV* points the way for ship owners. The works of other authors had some influence: for example, Poul Anderson's world-building was inspirational for many involved in shaping CT; David Drake's "Hammer's Slammers" stories of galactic mercenaries (collected 1979) probably contributed to the combined role-playing/war gaming found in CT's *Mercenary* (1978); and so on, down to the possibility that perhaps CT's emperor "Cleon I" is the sole minutia mined from Asimov's *Foundation*. But these traces can hardly be weighed against the elements from Tubb and Piper.

Traveller **and the history of SF (1965 to 2001)**
CT offered a new form of sf, where hard sf mixed with noir situations, offering easy, deadly violence. CT achieved all of this within the realm of rpgs, establishing a brand that was the reigning standard for several years, yet this success did not trigger a "hard noir" or "spaghetti sf" in written sf. To examine CT's legacy within the context of written sf, it is necessary to sketch out four different sf periods: New Wave, Star Wars, Cyberpunk, and Millennial Fever.

New Wave period (1965–1977). The sf New Wave was a literary infusion of the "juvenile" genre. On the one hand this meant more adult-themed material (including sex and violence), and the sense that sf was "finally growing up." But on the other hand, there was a move away from hard sf to soft sf, as well as an abandonment of space adventure in favor of inner space psychedelia. This gap is where CT later created its niche.

One of the milestones for the New Wave is Harlan Ellison's "Dangerous Visions" series of anthologies. *Dangerous Visions* (1967) had sold an incredible 50,000 copies in hardcover (plus 45,000 book club copies) by the time *Again, Dangerous Visions* (1972) went to press.

Star Wars period (1977–1983), from *Star Wars* (1977) to *Return of the Jedi* (1983). The first movie was the number 1 top grossing film for 20 years (squeezed out by *Titanic* in 1997), and the other two are in the top ten as well. This is a cultural phenomenon much larger than the genre community, and its arrival effectively spelled the end of the New Wave.

Star Wars represented a return to the "juvenile" form of sf. Like CT, it was a space adventure rejection of New Wave, with a certain grittiness in machinery, and something of a noir-hero in Han Solo. But *Star Wars* also rejected hard sf and went in the direction of 1930s-era blasters and space opera, which CT had avoided. (It is also noteworthy that the "Star Wars" movies followed the D&D model: the hero is a young, unskilled farm boy who acquires skills and powers in the course of his adventure; i.e., he essentially "goes up a level" from time to time. This is the opposite of CT, where characters go through a career, get skills, and then go adventuring without getting further improvement.)

CT was boosted along, despite the differences. The sf movies of the period that come closest to CT are the "Mad Max" series and *Blade Runner*. *Mad Max* (1979), *Mad Max 2: the Road Warrior* (1981), and (slightly out of period) *Mad Max Beyond Thunderdome* (1985) are morally ambiguous and violent, but set in the anarchy of a post-apocalyptic Earth. *Blade Runner* (1982) is film noir to the point of retro-stylings, the technology is a good fit for CT (the "spinners" are CT grav cars; Deckard's pistol is CT's "body pistol"), and while the story is Earth-bound, there are hints of off-world colonies and interstellar warfare.

Cyberpunk period (1983–1992), from Jedi to Clinton. Written sf finally went noir, embracing hardboiled sentiments, criminal activity, and easy violence, all part of the CT mix. But contrary to CT, Cyberpunk was never about space adventure; in fact, its signature "brain/computer interface" notion, taken from Delany's award-winning space adventure *Nova* (1969), was just a fresh coat of paint on the New Wave's "inner space."

During this time, CT was revised as *MegaTraveller* (1986–1991).

Millennial Fever period (1992–2001), from Clinton to September 11th. The USSR fell without a nuclear apocalypse, a miracle that took some years to see out. The arrival of the Internet spelled the end of Cyberpunk, and the "post-industrial economy," a dead pipe-dream of the 1980s, suddenly seemed to be coming true with the Internet's new economy (Cyberpunk's scary "megacorps" had morphed into warm-and-fuzzy "dot com" start-ups). The coming of the new millennium furthered the feeling of "newness" and transcendence: Vernor Vinge's "singularity" (the near future "event horizon" of magical technology) being a perfect icon of this sf eschatology/evolution.

The "Baroque Space Opera" of Vinge's award-winning *A Fire Upon the Deep* (1992) brought another surge of hard sf, but along with it came that pesky space opera. In addition, it seemed at times as though the "hard sf" had been completely co-opted by the New Wave: nanotech, biotech, smart dust, personality uploads, grey goo, post-humans ... all the "new" signs and symbols were outside the scope of *Traveller*.

Traveller: the New Era (1992) replaced *MegaTraveller*. The gaming company GDW ceased to exist in 1995, but *Traveller* itself sprouted up in new places: *Marc Miller's Traveller*, or "T4" (1996–1998), *GURPS Traveller* (1996 and currently), and *T20* (2002 and currently).

In media sf, the best approximation of CT appeared at this very late point in the form of an anime TV series and movie from Japan: *Cowboy BeBop* (1998). Noir and stylish, it features: space adventure; real brand-name guns in space; money-grubbing bounty hunters struggling to get enough money for their next meal; streetwise connections; combat enhancing drugs; shady alliances; double-crossing; treasure hunting; and more "hard sf" than just about any other anime to date.

Traveller was a vision powerful enough to dominate the sfrpg world, but never strong enough to break out of that niche. Written sf has cycled through three movements in the decades since *Traveller* was published, yet none of them were quite the "hard noir" blend that *Traveller* represents. Despite this, *Traveller* endures as a sturdy creation inspired by war gaming and noir adventure, built upon a solid foundation of lesser-known sf texts.

Works Cited

GDW. *Adventure 6: Expedition to Zhodane*. Game Designers' Workshop, 1981.

———. *Double Adventure 1: Shadows/Annic Nova*. GDW, 1979.

———. *Double Adventure 2: Across the Bright Face/Mission on Mithril*. GDW, 1979.

———. *Journal of the Travellers' Aid Society* issues 2, 3, and 4 (1979)

———. *Supplement 1: 1001 Characters*. GDW, 1978.

———. *Supplement 3: The Spinward Marches*. GDW, 1979.

———. *Supplement 4: Citizens of the Imperium*. GDW, 1979.

———. *Supplement 6: 76 Patrons*. GDW, 1980.

———. *Traveller, Deluxe Edition*. GDW, 1981.

Piper, H. Beam. *Space Viking*. Ace Science Fiction: New York. 1983.

———. *Uller Uprising*. Ace, 1983.

Tubb, E.C. *The Jester at Scar*. Ace, 1982.

———. *Jondelle*. Arrow: London, 1977.

———. *Kalin*. Arrow: London, 1976.

———. *Lallia*. Ace, 1982.

———. *Toyman*. Ace, 1982.

———. *The Winds of Gath*. Ace, 1982.

DECIPHERING THE TEXTS... ADDITIONS, ELABORATIONS

A few words in 2020 about the 2005 article.

In a game shop I frequented in the 1980s I had heard observations on the connection between CT and Dumarest. While I had not read Dumarest, I could see the similarities between CT and H. Beam Piper's fiction. An article on the links between CT and fiction seemed like the sort of thing that should be written, in fact it seemed odd to me that it had not already been written, since it seemed to be common knowledge. So, decades later, I set out to do it.

Poul Anderson

When I wrote "Poul Anderson's world-building was inspirational for many involved in shaping CT," I meant the hard science side of planetary size, gravity, atmosphere, and details like that, rather than the cultural side. I was trying to carve-out that angle for Anderson, as well as avoiding an "everything but the kitchen sink" sort of listing.

"Traveller: 2300"

On the topic of "Traveller: 2300" as a prequel to CT, I should have written a bit more or not mentioned it at all.

In 2005 this was addressed in the article's online comments

section, where one reader wrote:

> *Just a nitpick: Traveller 2300 was never part of the Classic Traveller universe, it just had the word "traveller" in the title and many people jumped to the obvious conclusion, which is why they changed it to 2300AD in the second edition.*

Here is my response:

Granted the "Traveller 2300" situation is confusing, and I wanted to treat it very lightly so as not to get bogged down, but I thought it was somewhat more confusing than your explanation.

That is, I dimly recall some early magazine articles by GDW people that introduced the game as a Traveller game (along the lines of how to integrate it and/or convert old Traveller into this new form). I don't think this was the article "Prologue—Adventure in the Not So Far Future" (on "backdating your Traveller campaign") from *Journal of the Travelers' Aid Society #20,* but that title is very suggestive of what I'm talking about.

I could be misremembering the alleged article, but at the very least, this sort of thing was in the air in 1984–85: a near-future Traveller campaign; a more "hard sf" approach or reinvention. Coming not from the fans but from the publisher.

I'm not so sure that the confusion was limited to the consumers, but I acknowledge that this has been asserted by GDW people after the fact. (I don't mean to be cryptic: it seems like there were a number of missteps in "MegaTraveller," "Traveller 2300"/"2300 AD," and "Traveller: the New Era"; branching out into "Space: 1889" was also a questionable move, in my opinion.)

My sense is that the name "Traveller: 2300" was a bungle somewhat akin to "New Coke" (1985).

Other Media S-F Approximating Traveller

In 2006, a reader commented:

> *A year late to the party, but another example of media SF that very closely approximates CT is the Firefly/Serenity verse.*

Here is my reply:

Yes, that's a good call. There are many points in *Firefly* (2002) that seem very much like CT: drugs, psionics, guns, starships, and most importantly, the "grey area" jobs of salvage and smuggling. CT never did the Western angle, which is good since *Firefly* is the one case in a thousand where it actually works! The Alliance is not much like canonical CT Imperium, but eh.

Alas, the fate of *Firefly* shows that the world *still* might not be ready for the basic concept.

While we're at it, the remake of *Battlestar Galactica* (2004) is another CT candidate (just add "High Guard" and "Robots"!), and seems to be faring better than *Firefly*.

It seems like Whedon has been very cagey about naming the sfrpg he used to play, but it sure seems to have been CT.

Psionics

Somewhere online, perhaps on reddit, a reader wished that I would treat CT's Psionics. I do so now.

I do not have much. The teleportation power is pure Edgar Rice Burroughs to me, from the Barsoom novels. The first level, where the person is transported without external materials, even clothing, is exactly what happens to John Carter in *A Princess of Mars* (1912) and Ulysses Paxton in *The Mastermind of Mars* (1928). The second level (teleportee clothed and able to carry a maximum 1 kg of cargo) is not addressed, but the third level (teleportee clothed and able to carry a full load) seems to be what John Carter is capable of in the fifth Barsoomian novel, *Chessmen of Mars* (1922), when he teleports to Earth through his own volition.

Notes From An Insider

In 2012 I was contacted by a person who had worked at GDW. I won't give a name.

It was interesting to get feedback from an insider. Most of my guesses were validated, but I learned a few surprises.

One surprise was that the CT supplement *76 Patrons* drew from *The Rockford Files* TV show. I had no idea, but it makes obvious sense, and it certainly adds to my "noir" stack.

I was surprised to find I was wrong about the "growler" from *Ranger* (an adventure for *2300 AD*). In the article I had expressed my conviction it was from H. Beam Piper's *Uller Uprising,* since that inter-mouth device is such a solid little dingus and I haven't seen it anywhere else in SF. That is, the tool isn't as widespread as a ray gun or blaster, rendering it generic. The GDW insider assured me that *Uller Uprising* was completely unknown at GDW. Together we wracked our brains and bent the Internet trying to track down another possible story with such an item, but we came up with nothing.

Our email discussion led me to expound upon the historical development of morality systems in role-playing games, forming the next essay.

MORALITY SYSTEMS IN ROLE-PLAYING GAMES

The complex topic of morality in Classic Traveller reminds me of a very short article in *White Dwarf #34* (1982) titled "Morality in *Traveller*." Writer Bob McWilliams opines that "*Traveller* referees may sometimes wish that players and non-player characters had some sort of restricting mechanism regarding their ethics, morality, state of grace, or whatever." To illustrate the point, he describes a *Traveller* game session where a mercenary platoon commander is sickened by how his third squad had slaughtered defenseless natives, so he swiftly orders a court martial and sends medics to tend the natives. Later that day, the platoon's advance has ground to a halt again, but the third squad leader has a native in custody who is known to have information on enemy positions. The native is frightened and disoriented, but he refuses to help the mercenaries. The commander orders the third squad leader to take the native out back and get the information, "I don't care how you do it."

The point is defining the player character's morality so that it can be accurately played by the player and understood as "in character" by the others (including the referee), so that he isn't a nice guy in the morning and a villain in the afternoon. There is no mention of the *Dungeons & Dragons* alignment system, but surely that is the context—as much as we might complain about the "lawful, neutral, chaotic" and "good, evil" descriptors, that is one of the ways that D&D forges a consensus on morality. (The other way is through the archetype nature of the character classes themselves: a paladin will act a certain way; a thief will act a certain way; and so on.)

For the CT article, McWilliams sketches out a solution of sorts, wherein a "Moral Code" number is chosen by the player at character creation. The scale is from one to six, with one being "the depths of moral depravity" and six "being saintly."

> On reaction throws, the referee compares the morality values of the two characters and uses the difference as a DM... He can also use the value in a number of other ways, especially with NPCs, to determine the likely response to situations.

McWilliams presents an interesting patch, but he doesn't go on to say that, obviously, the Imperial Navy will skew toward the good side and the space pirates will skew toward the evil side. Which is to say, even CT has archetypal characters for many of the professions.

Along these same lines, morality within computer rpgs went through a series of changes, as evidenced through the *Ultima* series (1981–85), the post-apocalyptic game *Wasteland* (1988), and the post-apocalyptic *Fallout* series (1997–2008).

The *Ultima* series developed, over time, a system that worked fairly well. *Ultima II* (1982) and *Ultima III* (1983) were both amoral, with lots of stealing and bad boy stuff along with the guilt-free slaughter of orcs and whatnot. (I never played *Ultima I*, but it was probably the same, just a little weaker. Things tend to build.) In *Ultima IV* (1985) it took a turn towards Arthurian principles, with the goal of becoming a "knight of virtue," which is why it developed the morality system. It seemed a bit nanny-ish, but that might be a necessary side-effect of the Arthurian principles.

In contrast, the post-apocalyptic game *Wasteland* (1988) took a non-moral approach, fitting to the grittiness of the situation. I found the lack of a nanny system to be refreshing, "realistic," and more "adult," but I think the developers were subsequently appalled by the "super munchkin" tactics of some players, best summarized by a published review that maximized experience points by slaughtering an entire village, etc. (The context being that in *Wasteland* you were supposed to be Desert Rangers, helping people, being "the good guys.") And Ken St. Andre, who was part of the design group, was not too happy with that "kill them all, rack up the points" approach.

When the people who had made *Wasteland* made a sequel, *Fallout* (1997), they put in a morality system. Basically, you start the game at neutral: if you do good things, you get a certain number of "Good Karma" points, and this becomes a general reputation as well as a reputation specific to each faction/community; if you do bad things, you get "Evil Karma." And you could do really bad things—kill children, sell people into slavery, etc. Some cases of stealing affect Karma in a negative way. There is also bad behavior that is not keyed to Karma, including prostitution, pimping (that is, you can force your wife into prostitution for money), alcohol use, drug use (performance enhancing chemicals like CT's Combat, etc.), drug addiction, double dealing, backstabbing, and so on. *Fallout* was so dark in this way that even the worldly French got upset.

It seems to me that the game designers learned the lesson of *Wasteland* and said, "Okay, you can be as wicked as you want, but there will be consequences."

Then something different happened in *Fallout 3* (2008) where it became dangerous to be "too good" or "too evil," as you would then be repeatedly ambushed by different factions. So in *Fallout 3* "studied neutrality" came into its own. Put another way, this amounts to "Don't stick out or you'll get hammered down." This means balancing out good deeds with bad deeds. This is quite interesting since it brings a "sweet spot" into the gritty gray area between light and dark. Such a strategy enhances the "noir" aspect.

Which is to say, it all comes down to *The Good, the Bad, and the Ugly* (1966). That old spaghetti Western nailed it: "neutral" is "ugly," but it is where most people are.

So what *Fallout* did, in essence, was take something like McWilliams's Moral Code and flesh it out with a laundry list of activities that would raise or lower a player character's moral rating by fractional increments. The difference in the two systems being that McWilliams's is a prescriptive one (the character must live according to his code, and it is locked down at character creation), whereas in *Fallout* the system is a descriptive one subject to constant change (the character's rating rises and falls due to his actions).

My sense is that GDW went through a somewhat similar track: that originally it was all wide open, but then the realities of "super munchkins" brought an increasing sense of morality in GDW products to establish "why it is okay to kill certain people." That is, the anarchy of a fantasy RPG actually has certain moral templates built in; a SF RPG lacks this basic grounding, so that the anarchy more closely resembles the turbulent 1970s.

I don't know why the designers of *Fallout* added a morality system to their game, but I can certainly guess and have done so. It may not be enough to warrant a distinction, but it seems to me that presenting the darker side as a career path (rather than a losing "dead end") is sort of the "anti-nanny" way, such that the full spectrum of nanny/anti-nanny matches the standard angel/devil on the shoulder.

LANGUAGES OF THE DYING SUN

Among novels set in the far future of Earth there are some that are placed near the very end, in the realm of the dying sun. These "dying sun" novels are neither science fiction nor fantasy but a hybrid form that combines the strengths of the two: science fantasy. The strategy of science fantasy represents a breaking away from the familiarities of its parent genres: it will rationalize a legendary monster on the one hand, only to make a mundane technological device seem magical on the other. The dying sun novel requires a vast human history, the rise and fall of countless civilizations, even if this is only implied in the vaguest terms. More important than the history itself is the effect of this history on the world: how the language has been shaped. This creates the "time gulf," the necessary vastness between the reader's world and the world of the text.

There were several precursors to the current form of the dying sun novel. On the science fiction side, H. G. Wells offered a glimpse of the red sun in *The Time Machine* (1895), but it was only a glimpse; another brief view was in the frame tale of Olaf Stapledon's *Last and First Men* (1930), a vision that is vast, in fact too vast for human characters, with narration that is stylistically dry. On the fantasy side, William Hope Hodgson's *The Night Land* (1912), set in the world after the sun has died, is told in a doubly archaic voice which finally overwhelms it; Clark Ashton Smith's "Zothique" stories (1932–1948) have many of the essential elements, but the stories are not linked together, in fact it seems that no two are even set in the same decade.

Putting all these together, then: what was needed was a sustained narrative, set in the land of the dying sun, with a style neither too dry nor too archaic (nor too lurid?), and a story that brings stellar mortality down to a human scale without losing the awe and mystery of the cosmic event.

Three exemplary novels are *The Dying Earth* (1950) by Jack Vance, *The Book of the New Sun* (1983) by Gene Wolfe, and *The Black Grail* (1986) by Damien Broderick. Each brings a different perspective: Vance creates the form, Wolfe pushes it to its fantasy edge, and Broderick drives it to its science fiction limit.

The Dying Earth

> *Turjan hesitated, then opened his eyes. It was night in white-walled Kaiin, and festival time ... Here was a Melantine bargeman, here a warrior of Valdaran's Green Legion, here another of ancient times wearing one of the old helmets. In a little cleared space a garlanded courtesan of the Kauchique littoral danced the Dance of the Fourteen Silken Movements to the music of flutes ... a girl barbarian of East Almery embraced a man blackened and in leather harness as a Deodand of the forest. They were gay, these people of waning Earth, feverishly merry, for infinite night was close at hand, when the sun should finally flicker and go black. (The Dying Earth, p.14)*

In Jack Vance's *The Dying Earth* the sun is so ill that people think it could go out at any moment. Vance is not concerned with how or why this is, nor with fixing the problem, nor even with witnessing the apocalypse when the sun goes dark: for Vance it is a state that provides a certain amount of background tension, and that is all (in a similar way Vance uses Lyonesse, a legendary place said to have sunk beneath the waves, as the setting for his *Lyonesse* fantasy trilogy). The Earth is facing certain extinction and humanity responds primarily with fatalistic resignation. Idle pleasures are pursued: wizardry, roguery, and robbery are the order of the waning day.

Yet throughout the six stories that make up TDE there is a quiet drive among heroic individuals to prepare for the universal death by rediscovering the human animal and all of its lost accomplishments. In "Turjan of Miir" the hero is working to make synthetic humans, not monsters, but humans at their best. With "Mazirian the Magician," Turjan's synthetic woman T'sain shows her heroic qualities by rescuing him from Mazirian (a monster-maker) at the cost of her own life. In "T'sais" another synthetic woman seeks to overcome the flaw in her design that makes her see the world as an ugly and horrible place: she seeks a cure, she seeks Truth and Beauty. On a quest for lost magic the dark urbanite "Ulan Dhor" meets a threat from the past in the form of a megalomaniac awakened from suspended animation. The bright country squire "Guyol of Sfere," searching for lost knowledge, finds the Museum of Man under siege by the demon Blikdak—and by ending the ancient siege he gains access to vast knowledge, the boon of the past.

These quests are seen as noble and they are rewarded with success. A certain amount of roguery is permitted the questers, but those who engage in torture and/or wanton murder (Mazirian the Magician, Liane the Wayfarer, Rogol Domedonfors) are perceived as villains and summarily dispatched in the course of the book. Thus, even though the end of the Earth is nigh, there is no license for anyone to make life into a hell on Earth. (This is in strong contrast to Clark Ashton Smith's "Zothique" stories, which revel in decadence and horror under a dying sun.)

The Dying Earth presents a fantasy surface (comparable to the work of Lord Dunsany) underpinned with scientific method (very unlike Dunsany); combined, this produces something rather like Edgar Rice Burroughs's Barsoom, moved from present Mars to far future Earth. In terms of style, TDE is light and bright, again very much like Dunsany and in strong contrast to Clark Ashton Smith (whose work is rather dark and heavy).

In the background of TDE is a cloudy history that sometimes breaks into the foreground. An age or more before the time of the book there existed a unified state known as Grand Motholam, in an era that bred the greatest magicians. At that time the sun was healthy and there were a thousand magical spells, but by the time of TDE the sun is dying and the number of spells has fallen to one hundred: thus, the contrast between a bright age of plenty and a dark age of scarcity. While an "age" is a relatively vague period of time, the scale continues to expand in the course of the book: the fifth story features a city under a curse for 5,000 years; the sixth story mentions a city abandoned for 10,000 years, and toward the end Kerlin the curator gasps about the lost time of his own bewitchment, "Now I remember the years and centuries, the millennia, the epochs—they are like quick glimpses through a shutter" (p. 150). [note 1]

As a large part of his science fantasy technique, Vance uses archaic words, faux-archaic words, and coinages to create TDE. Here are some examples from geography: Grand Motholam (p. 29) is the name of the region where the stories take place, and includes provinces Ascolais, Almery, Kauchique; the rivers Derna and Scaum; Tenebrosa Bay and the Bay of Sanreale; the Fer Aquila Mountains; and the oddities Embelyon (a land not of the same place) and Ampridatvir (a city not of the same time). Grand Motholam is a fairy tale Europe: the Land of the Falling Wall is to the East, just as China stands with its Great Wall (or as the Caucus Mountains with its "Iron Gates" of Derbend).

I trace "Motholam" to "motho," obsolete form of motto (OED), hence "motto-land," hinting at heraldry (heraldic mottoes), fiefdoms, and a checkerboard landscape of "isms" (alluded to in Vance's *Houses of Iszm*). Ascolais is perhaps derived from "ascolia" (the second day of a rural Dionysia); Almery is an obsolete form of "ambry" (a repository or place for keeping things; a storehouse, a treasury; a cupboard). Located somewhere to the west, the name of exotic Kauchique looks like "Zothique" (and "antique") but it may be closer to "caucho," the rubber produced in the Amazon basin and Central America (to the west of Europe). The River Derna might flow from "derne," obsolete form of "dernly" (secretly); the river Scaum certainly comes from "scaum" (a thin haze or mist; a light, misty vapor). The Latin roots of Tenebrosa Bay ("tenebros") means dark; the Bay of Sanreale recalls "sang-royal" (royal blood) and the related typo that launched a thousand quests (sangrail). "Fer Aquila" looks like Latin "wild eagle," a good name for a group of mountains.

Then there is the otherworldly Embelyon, a place that can only be reached through the Call to the Violent Cloud, which carries the magician "four directions, then one": surely this derives from "embelief," the obsolete astronomical term meaning "in an oblique direction; oblique." "Ampridatvir" seems derived from "amritattva" a Sanskrit word for immortality, which serves well to depict the stasis-sleep of Rogol Domedonfors, and his virtual immortality as a disembodied cyborg-brain. It also has a certain similarity to Amritsar, the city in Punjab: the names are close; Amritsar was founded by Ram Das (sharing initials with Rogol Domedonfors), and the Golden Temple is prominent (Rogol Domedonfors is hidden in the tower with a yellow dome); to the Euro-centric viewpoint it is ancient, exotic, and rife with religious conflict (all fitting for the city described in the book). But Ampridatvir is placed to the northwest, in a location rather more like Ireland as seen from Europe.

The character names are for the most part more obscure in their meaning, largely coinages of a form remarkably similar to those names dreamed up by Clark Ashton Smith. Turjan the Magician does not seem very "turgid," but maybe more like "turgeman," obsolete form of "truchman" (an interpreter). Pandelume's flawed synthetic woman T'sais might be "the sixth" creation (Spanish *seis*) or French "ya know" (*t'sais*); but Turjan's corrected version, T'sain, is both "the sane" and healthy (French *sain*) in contrast. Then there is Ulan Dhor, whose name rings with crystal clarity: "ulan" being horseman (from Turkish) and "dhor" from *dhu* meaning black (in Celtic). The character is introduced as "a slender young man, pale of skin, with the blackest of hair, eyes, and eyebrows" (p. 80); he sails across the Melantine (again, "dark")

Gulf. Guyal, who is the very picture of the innocent quester (like Parsifal), still manages to use "guile" to win the day. Kerlin the Curator of the Museum of Man echoes Merlin the magician not only in name and alliteration, but also in being bewitched into a kind of stasis.

The Dying Earth has a number of strange creatures that seem drawn from fairy tale logic. The Twk-men, tiny humanoids who ride dragonflies and sell information for salt (the name perhaps related to "twke," the obsolete Scottish past-tense of "take"). And the dread Deodand, like black elves or trolls, man-sized, urbane and cunning, enamored of human flesh. The word "deodand" is a legal term in English law for a thing responsible for a person's death that is forfeited to the Crown to be applied to pious uses (thus the "deo" part of the word). But in dry Vancean humor, forget the pious uses and forget the Crown, this creature is a thing responsible for a person's death.

Despite the general look and feel of fantasy, there are science fictional elements present from the first page (for example, synthetic humans are being made in "vats" rather than alchemical vessels). In the final third of the book the technological gains an edge over the magical as the heroes encounter ancient science-cum-magics: the ruined city Ampridatvir has devices identical to such sf hardware as slidewalks ("flowing roadway," "gliding strip"), grav tubes ("shaft of No-weight"), groundcars ("magic cars"), and aircars ("air-boats"); the Museum of Man has countless computers ("banks," "great brains"). Vance further signals this change in emphasis with words of his own invention, in the style of traditional science fiction (or a parody thereof). Thus we have "audiarium" (p. 145) as office (or office hours, or hearing chamber); "cerebrologist" (p. 146) instead of psychiatrist (which, being a twentieth century term, would simply ruin everything); "corolpsis" (p. 82); "metathasm" (p. 82); "potentium" (p. 149) rather than atomic power plant; "sometsyndic" (p. 146) instead of neurological; "superphysic numeration" (p. 82) instead of transuranic elements. There are also some job titles, for example "the Lycurgat" (p. 145), apparently a kind of supreme ruler (derived from Lycurgus, traditional lawgiver and founder of the Spartan constitution), and "the Voyevode" (p. 124), ruler of Saponce (related to the obsolete, rare word "voye" meaning "way"; hence "master of the way" for the road between Saponce and the Museum of Man).

By using these terms, many of them coinages built with archaic parts, Vance is able to steal the fire of science fiction without using the standard mid-twentieth century science-fictional terminology: thus the "time gulf," so necessary to the subgenre, is maintained by excluding twentieth century words whenever possible.

[note 1]
Historical Points for *The Dying Earth*
Grand Motholam: bright age.
21st Aeon, the Age of the Dying Sun: dark age.
    Carchasel city abandoned: 10,000 years before TDE.
    Ampridatvir city cursed: 5,000 years before TDE.
    The setting of *The Dying Earth.*

(note: "21st Aeon" is given in *Rhialto the Marvellous* (1984), a later work set on the dying Earth.)

The Book Of The New Sun

> *A moment suffices to describe these things, for which I watched so long. The decades of a saros would not be long enough for me to write all they meant to the ragged apprentice boy I was. Two thoughts (that were nearly dreams) obsessed me and made them infinitely precious. The first was that at some not-distant time, time itself would stop [...] the colored days that had so long been drawn forth like a chain of conjuror's scarves would come to an end, the sullen sun wink out at last. The second was that there existed somewhere a miraculous light—which I sometimes conceived of as a candle, sometimes as a flambeau—that engendered life*

in whatever objects it fell upon. (The Shadow of the Torturer, p. 22)

Where Vance treats his dying sun as a natural and unalterable condition, Gene Wolfe takes a different track with his work *The Book of the New Sun*. The title itself promises at least the hope of a solution to the problem of a dying sun, and over the course of four volumes it becomes clear that the sun's condition is not the natural result of stellar evolution (instead a small black hole has been put into it) and that while a technological fix is possible, it will be neither easy nor pain-free (in fact it will result in mass extinction, the death of the old world).

So in a sense Wolfe provides more science fictional scaffolding for the dying sun motif, but the way he does this is by increasing the fantasy content by diving more deeply into forgotten words rather than coinages. Furthermore, the old words that Wolfe uses often come with most of their baggage intact. "Urth" is the name of the planet where the story takes place, and while the name is a homonym of "Earth," it is also the name for the Norse norn of the past. The setting of the first volume is the vast city Nessus, named after a centaur who appears in both Greek mythology (he poisoned Heracles) and in Dante's *Inferno* (he ferries Dante across one of the rivers). The River Gyoll, which runs through all four volumes, is named after a river of death in Norse mythology.

Wolfe uses standard sf terms like "laser" and "hologram" very sparingly. More often he uses a substitution with simple medieval sensibilities: solar cells become "the black plates that drink the sun" (II, p. 204); the black hole becomes "the black worm that devours the sun" (II, p. 33); robot (20th century word) is changed into the older word "android" (18th century word); synthetic humanoid is replaced with "homunculus." Where Wolfe really begins to shine is with the stranger words: clone becomes "khaibit" (ancient Egyptian word for "shadow self"); hyperspace and normal-space become "Yesod" and "Briah" (terms for different universes in the Kabbalah of Jewish mysticism). Then there are the pyrotechnic pole arms, where exotic technology meets archaic terminology: contus, hastarus, demilune, and more. This is a case of Wolfe using old words for new things, following a poetic logic that sings the frightful beauty of terrible weaponry.

Here is a different case, where the common is made strange: In the torture chamber (I, ch. 12) are a number of devices from history and literature (see the apparatus from Kafka's "In the Penal Colony"), yet the one selected to punish Thecla is the revolutionary, a machine that uses electric shock to awaken an indwelling demon within the victim. This demon causes the victim to constantly hurt herself, eventually causing self-blindness and ultimately, after about a month, death. In other words, the revolutionary is an electro-shock therapy device that instils suicidal depression rather than removing the same. Such a thing seems implausible, impossible; since we know that sane people are not made insane by electrical shock. But a moment of magical thinking shows that suicidal depression can be seen as an entity which cannot be destroyed, it can only be sent away; so the twentieth century machine is the "sending" device, and the torturers' machine is the "receiving" device: mental illness has been teleported to the end of history.

There are very few coinages in TBOTNS. One, "Naviscaput," is the name of a monster which serves to describe it as well (Latin "boat" and "head"; "boat-head," for an aquatic creature). Another example is the "avern," an extraterrestrial flower: its name derives from Avernus, a lake in Italy considered an entrance to the Underworld in ancient times, and the fictional flower is found in just such a place, if not exactly the same place (since the botanical gardens of Nessus might bend through time and space). There is a complete lack of coinage in character names; instead there is a pattern: enemies of the New Sun have the names of ancient monsters (Abaia, Erebus, Arioch, Typhon, etc.), mortals have names of Christian saints (Abban, Abundantius, Agia, Agilus, etc.), aliens have names of classical gods and sibyls (Ossipago, Barbatus, Famulimus, the Cumaean). Exceptions to the rule reveal even more about a character: Jonas (from Jonah, the Jewish prophet) turns out to be from an age prior to the Age of the Autarch. The bestiary of Urth includes a large number of prehistoric creatures (uintather, tyrannosaur, trilophon, thylacosmil, etc.) mixed in with some mythological creatures (alzabo, peryton, salamander, etc.).

All of these strategies work to create the time gulf, and a further separation of high tech and medieval tech within the world itself adds to the implication of a vast period of time dividing the reader's world from the world of the dying sun. In keeping with the medieval world-view, Wolfe blurs the sense of time, moving away from the clock-bound, work week, calendar-driven machine of the modern world. On Urth there are no hours, there are "watches," which are seasonally variable; there are weeks, but no named days of the week; years are reckoned by the reign of the current autarch; and so on. But then he slyly does something else: he removes the ancient cultural concepts "sunrise" and "sunset," replacing them with phrases acknowledging that it is the Urth who turns her face toward the sun and away from the sun: "the west was lifted to cover the sun" (I, p. 130); "Urth's laboring margin has climbed once more above the red disk" (II, p. 209); "Urth had turned almost her full face to the sun" (III, p. 293). Soft and subtle, yet this shows a culture which has finally incorporated the Copernican Revolution and maintains this as a stubborn relic even as decline has returned it to a medieval level.

Wolfe presents a fantasy surface dotted with science fictional artifacts (e.g., rocket ships serving as castle towers), beneath which lurk mysteries of both science and religion. Pushing the morality of TDE a bit further, TBOTNS seeks to change a professional torturer into some kind of redemptive hero. All this is done in a baroque style comparable to Clark Ashton Smith or Mervyn Peake.

The history of Urth is divided into four ages. The future age, like Schrodinger's Cat, exists as two mutually exclusive potentials: the dead state of Ragnarok (named for the Final Winter of Norse myth) and the live state of Ushas (the name of a Hindu dawn goddess). If the new sun does not come, then Ragnarok will be realized; if the new sun arrives, Urth will be destroyed and reborn as Ushas. So while the reason for the sun's dying condition remains veiled, by the end of TBOTNS the probability of a new sun arriving seems to be a fairly comforting likelihood of somewhere between fifty and ninety-five percent. [note 2]

Through this tour-de-force strategy Wolfe creates a rich mosaic made up of forgotten words—names, creatures, weapons, and more. They work their magic, they all seem so real in part because they are real words. The end result is an obscuring of the "science fictional" and an embellishing of the "fantastical," making TBOTNS a science fantasy that goes to the fantasy edge.

[note 2]
Historical Points for *The Book of the New Sun*
Age of Myth: location of reader.
Age of the Monarch: time of the galactic empire.
Age of the Autarch: setting of TBOTNS.
Age of Ushas/Ragnarok: the two potential futures.

The Black Grail

> *Pinpoints of blinding light, two in the west and two at the eastern horizon, blazed bright as boiling iron. I blinked my shocked gaze away from them, and for a moment saw only the pinpoint images of blackness which clung to my eyes.... I forced myself to look finally at the quadrant of the heavens between those high, fierce chariots of light.*
>
> *I had not recognized what I saw, not at once. Now I did.*
>
> *Midday-high, vast as a cartwheel, sullen as an ancient god flecked with black cancer, loomed the coal-red ember of the dying sun. (The Black Grail, p. 38)*

Damien Broderick's *The Black Grail* (1986) has a curious history of its own: it is a revised and expanded version of his earlier novel *Sorcerer's World* (1970). Thus it mostly predates Wolfe's TBOTNS and is, like TBOTNS, a response to Vance's TDE. There is a literary angle, too: the dedication of the Australian edition ("For my mother and father these revised new syllables") is a direct pointer to *Giles Goat-Boy: or, the Revised New Syllabus* (1966) by John Barth.

This requires a bit of unpacking. *Giles Goat-Boy* is a massive send-up of campus life and the campus novel, so we might expect TBG to be a parody of the dying sun novel. But the parody it contains is gentle, and mainly self-directed (that is, toward *Sorcerer's World*); in the main TBG is a distinctive and original novel in the dying sun tradition.

A strange thing had happened in the decades following the publication of Vance's TDE: science and science writers began taking the idea seriously for a variety of reasons. The geological record seemed to be showing strange patterns of solar cooling which might be related to Ice Ages; experiments to find solar neutrinos had fallen short, raising questions as to whether fusion was actually going on in the sun or was it all just powered by a black hole? And why was the young sun so weak according to the fossil records? Meanwhile Arthur C. Clarke's famous "Third Law" ("Any sufficiently advanced technology is indistinguishable from magic") entered the science fictional dialogue as an important touchstone (*Profiles of the Future*, 1962), and engineers dreamed up stellar-scale projects, including techniques to extend the natural lifespan of the sun (by mining them) and ways to move planets into different orbits (1962: see Fogg's *Terraforming*).

Some of this likely played a part in forming Wolfe's TBOTNS. Broderick is very clear about it with TBG: he includes quotes from the science writings of Sir Fred Hoyle, Nigel Calder, and John Gribbin.

Broderick uses two future eras in telling TBG: the first is an ice age roughly one thousand years in the future; the second is the age of the Failing Sun, about a million years in the future. This device by itself serves as an excellent time gulf: the hero Xaraf Firebridge has grown up as a barbarian nomad in the future dark age, and then comes to be manipulated by the Powers of the later time. [note 3]

Broderick brings a solid science fictional surface to his dying sun novel. The Powers themselves speak clear and standard sf jargon, which goes somewhat over the hero's head but straight into the sf reader's: when they discover Xaraf among them, they fall to arguing and one remarks,

> "The clarity of our insights is doubtless marred by the not negligible effort of guiding a good portion of the sun's energy output across a time differential of some six thousand million years." (p. 28)

This immediately identifies them as engineers of time and space. The bickering continues: "Surely you do not imply that this uncouth lout has been drawn here along a temporal wormline from a million years in the past!" (p. 28).

The speech-patterns, the fact that they are arguing, their attitude toward the barbarian, all are very much like Vancean magicians, yet "temporal wormline" would never be used.

The Earth Xaraf encounters in the far future is a strange one indeed. The years seem to be twelve years long (p. 135), and in addition to the bloated red sun there are a number of Earth-warming sunlets, as the Powers explain:

> "When the sun swelled in its terminal convulsions, we shifted the world to a cooler orbit. We stripped the system's gas giants of their fuel and ignited them [as the Earth orbiting sunlets]." (p. 41)

In this manner the technical aspects of a dying sun are laid out. The sun grew giant, just as theory suggests it will, so the planet was moved out to the former orbit of ex-Jupiter (a little research shows this position has a twelve-year orbit). The sun's moribund condition is explained: "The sun has been dying ever since greedy humans discovered the wormline principle and gutted its core" (p. 76).

So the situation with the sun is one of a vast energy crisis, and the fluctuation of the sun's output over prehistoric time is thus explained. The Powers, in an attempt to find new resources with which to stabilize the sun, have hit upon the technocratic solution of tapping the prehistoric sun at the earliest possible moment, six billion years in the past: robbing the youth to extend the life of the old. But the arrival of Xaraf is an anomaly which suggests disaster: "Some other agency has gained entry to our wormlines" (p. 54).

The Powers are not alone in their use of science fiction language: Xaraf's home time period is also anchored in sf. In describing the time before his own, Xaraf writes:

> *"Before they destroyed themselves in the Holocaust, the mad men of the Black Time had built places all of metals, glass . . . these had melted in the fires of the Holocaust. We could not approach those poisoned craters." (p. 23)*

"The Black Time," "the fires of the Holocaust," "poisoned craters," all these belong to the lexicon of the post-apocalyptic genre, a body of fiction that brings its own set of nuances.

Xaraf's homeland is in an ice age: there are living glaciers (p. 46) in the Southern Hemisphere where he lives; the lifestyle of his tribe includes such details as hunting rhinos by running them off cliffs (p. 22)—a ice-age animal and an ice-age technique. The tribe uses baluchitheriums as riding mounts, again harkening to prehistoric times (by way of genetic reconstruction). (We note in passing that during an ice age the sea level drops as water is locked-up into ice; this in turn alters coastlines and exposes landbridges connecting Asia to North America as well as Australia.) But post-apocalyptic terminology puts a spin on all this: it seems quite likely that their ice age is really a "nuclear winter," yet Broderick does not have to say it explicitly—the implication is there. This is interesting because it makes the time gap between Xaraf and reader only paper thin, and widens the gulf between Xaraf and the Powers to an Astronomical Unit or more.

Even though the surface is science fictional, still the fantasy imagery seeps in all around. Instead of ray guns, there are swords —not even energy swords, just swords. There is the "quest," of course, which involves killing a world tyrant, freeing a princess, and obtaining the boon of immortality. The hero's advisors include a talking sword and a gryphon. In contrast to Vance and Wolfe, Broderick does not use a great number of archaic words: instead he uses tableaux and situations which are usually associated with fantasy works. In order to illustrate this I will have to rely more upon plot summary rather than the etymology of single words.

The three Powers themselves offer much for fantastic thought. Jesrilban Julix (a young man), Ah Balmorq (a battle-scarred mature man), and Eis Creid (an ancient man) seem easily identified with Son, Father, and Holy Ghost. But a closer analogy can be made with the three instructional beings "High," "Just-as-High," and "Third" in Snorri Sturluson's *The Deluding of Gylfi* (13th century). This may be of more than just passing similarity, since *The Deluding* involves a *Volkerwanderung,* colorful heroic quests, a *Götterdämmerung,* and then an abrupt implosion into "never-was-ness" because the telling of pagan myths in a Christianized Scandinavian world amounts to a "deluding."

The title of TBG ties it directly to the Grail Romance. At key points in the text there are dream-visions that use Set and Osirus from ancient Egyptian myth, and Gilgamesh and Enkidu from Sumerian myth, but through it all the primary focus seems to be from Arthurian Cycle.

The black grail itself is something of an anti-climax, almost a McGuffin. Xaraf is being trained by the Powers in preparation for his return to his own time, and his first quest involves finding the vanished city of Treet Hoown. Doing this he discovers a world tyrant in suspended animation, and with the tyrant (whose name is Aji-suki-takahikone) is Comrhia Cthain, a woman Xaraf knows from a series of dreams in his childhood. Xaraf learns that the tyrant, seeking the immortality that the Powers have, fought against them and lost: but now his entire city is an elaborate immortality-test. If anyone can survive the death ray called "Mysterium

Coniunctionis" (alchemical term for "union of opposites") and grasp the black grail, then the tyrant will be awakened from his 100,000-year stasis.

The lesson from the Powers to Xaraf seems to be "see our enemy, see our might, put him down (and we will give you what he wanted)," since in his next quest Xaraf gains immortality. The grail itself is little more than an ornate electrical switch. But it serves as a focus for the reader, and when we see the tableau through an Arthurian lens we are surprised to recognize the tyrant as King Pelles, the fisher king, and Comrhia Cthain as the grail maiden Blanchefleur (vanished true love of Percival), with Xaraf as Galahad and Percival combined (he gets the grail and the girl). Yet the victory is not a happy one, and then another quest presents itself.

Xaraf's immortality comes from an attempt to find a cure for Queen Aniera's wasting disease. Xaraf and Glade, his female warrior companion, travel to Haunt of Monsters, an adventure in which Gilgamesh's quest for gray-grow-young blends with Adam and Eve in Eden by way of Bosch's *Garden of Earthly Delights*. Glade is the first to eat their goal, the alien symbiote, but she vomits it up; Xaraf eats another and keeps it down. Then they have to fight their way off of the island of monstrous plants and animals, but by the time they return to Glade's city, the Queen has already died.

Once again the Powers seem to have been served. Xaraf is now their agent, readied: armed with a magic sword, trained in the magic technologies, and immortal. But he is always kept in the dark, he has become disheartened, he chafes under their puppet-mastery. They summon him for the last time, and here is a new mystery: for with the three he met before is a woman called Flowers of Evening whom he had known as a man named Darkbloom. His mentor.

Xaraf is sent back to his own time for the final battle. Glade elects to go with him. They meet his nemesis, Dragon: a saurian humanoid created by Darkbloom. Dragon reveals that the Powers in their relentless hunger for solar energy began tapping the sun after life had begun on Earth, thus knowingly causing all the ice ages and all of the mass extinctions of the world. Including, therefore, the quasi-nuclear winter of Xaraf's time (actually this one is caused by Dragon himself). The true battle is revealed to be not so much who wields the power of the sun, but rather, whose timeline is wiped out. The stakes are much higher, and suddenly it seems as though Xaraf is on the wrong side: the side of Evil.

But Xaraf fights as well as he can, and he loses. This is very surprising, needless to say, and yet suddenly the Arthurian circuit is complete: Xaraf as Arthur, losing the final battle; Darkbloom as Merlin, who had trained both Arthur and his enemy Vivian; Dragon as both Vivian, who betrayed Merlin, and Modred, who vanquished Arthur; and human existence on Earth as Logres. At the same time, Dragon is also Galahad as he claimed to be (p. 292), and the "grail" he has won, the ability to reproduce his own race of saurian humanoids, is the true grail of the novel, however downbeat it might be for humanity. A utopian world, yes, but a non-mammalian one, where Xaraf and Glade are something like Ash and Vine (post-Ragnarok Adam and Eve) in a Saurian zoo.

Broderick accomplishes all this with New Wave vigor (style comparable to Moorcock) and verve (use of quoted texts; parody/homage; use of sf references and in-jokes).

Foreign languages and language games are scattered throughout TBG. The name Xaraf is part joke, the reverse (and variant) spelling of Australian infant cereal "Farex" (in SW the hero's name was "Klim Xaraf of Tribe Tnafni"; thanks to Russell Blackford for the baby food reference); but it also seems to be part serious, read as "carafe," which is supported by the scene where Xaraf is carrying the symbiote in his stomach and Glade remarks, "I think you are a courier, my poor dear. A vessel. A living container" (p. 285). This seems like an important image for a book called the black grail.

Xaraf's father is "Golan," a name which invokes the modern warfare of the Golan Heights as well as the Biblical city of refugees. Xaraf names his talking sword "Alamogordo" ("a name from the depths of the Black Time . . . the weapon which all but burnt up the world," p. 73) after the birthplace of the atomic bomb. Xaraf's homeland is "Kravaard," which sounds appropriately icy, Scandinavian. Since there is a tradition in post-apocalyptic fiction of slurring or mutating the names of cities and regions ("Eusa" for USA, "Cambry" for Canterbury, in Hoban's *Riddley Walker;* "Clevelen" for Cleveland in Crowley's *Engine Summer*), we are invited to find real-place, Southern Hemisphere locations for Berb-Kisheh (North African "Berbers"?), Rokhmun (Rockingham, near Perth?), Rezot-Azer Valley ("resort azure"?), and Nazarokh (looks suspiciously like "Nazareth"). Then again, it is quite possible that all these locations are on land submerged in the twentieth century.

Late in the text we are told that Xaraf's mother's name is "Neeshyaya Yubka," which "means 'petticoat' in the old tongue" (p. 284). Some research reveals that this seemingly made-up name really does mean petticoat in Russian (*nyzhnyaya yubka*), with a little slurring. Knowing that the old language of the Wanderers is Russian suggests a vast *Volkerwanderung* from the steppes of the Northern Hemisphere to their lands in the Southern Hemisphere, a good fit with post-apocalyptic assumptions about Cold War legacies. (The other names from Xaraf's family have no Russian meaning I could find, but his sister's name, Babinya (p. 133), is Indonesian for "swine": and by coincidence or design, the Indonesian ice-age landbridge is the walking path from Russia to Australia). To return to place-names, perhaps the "Kisheh" of Berb-Kisheh is derived from Russian *kishyeh* (to swarm with, to teem with); and maybe "the wheeling Rokhmun thieves" (p. 10), tribal enemies of the Wanderers, owe their name to Russian *rokhly* (dawdler).

If Xaraf's ice age is a crypto-Russian period, then the Age of the Powers shows evidence of Japanese influence. The world tyrant's name, "Aji-suki-takahikone," looks unmistakably Japanese; and in fact, it turns out to be the name of an ancient Japanese thunder god. Putting these together, we see three stages of a post-Western Civilization world: Russian, Japanese, and the enigmatic, godlike Powers.

Broderick gives a complete and straightforward science fictional presentation of a dying sun scenario and introduces post-apocalyptic elements as well, taking the dying sun novel to its science fiction limit. But through his use of myth and archetype, the look and feel of fantasy still permeates: a gloomy, pessimistic, Scandinavian sort, the kind that forms the wellspring of Gylfi, Arthur, and Ragnarok. The hubris of the Powers results in a curse handed up to their remotest ancestors: the problem-solving aspect of science fiction is trumped by the Wyrd of fantasy.

[note 3]
Historical Periods of *The Black Grail*
6 billion years BCE: the feedpoint.
65 million years BCE: Cretaceous extinctions.
CE 2100: (circa) the Black Time, location of reader.
CE 3100: Xaraf's Ice Age.
CE 900,000: Treet Hoown abandoned.
CE 940,000: Haunt of Monsters on Earth.
CE 1,000,000: the time of the Failing Sun.

These three "dying sun" novels show the fusion of fantasy and science fiction into science fantasy. Clarke's Third Law insists upon technology seeming magical as the technology gap increases between observer and artifact, so to quest under the red sun, or to be born and live there in the far future, would seem to involve a great deal of such magical technology. As we have seen, these books use archaic words, faux-archaic coinages, myths and archetypes to achieve their goal, and together they form a fascinating conversation about humanity's place in the universe.

Bibliography

Broderick, Damien. *The Black Grail*. New York: Avon, 1986.
Vance, Jack. *The Dying Earth*. New York: Pocket Books, 1977.
Wolfe, Gene. *The Shadow of the Torturer*. New York: Simon

& Schuster, 1980.
———. *The Claw of the Conciliator.* New York: Simon & Schuster, 1981.
———. *The Sword of the Lictor.* New York: Simon & Schuster, 1981.
———. *The Citadel of the Autarch.* New York: Simon & Schuster, 1983.

Secondary Sources

Andre-Driussi, Michael. *Lexicon Urthus* (and supplements). P.O. Box 6248 Albany, California: Sirius Fiction, 1994.
Blackford, Russell. *Hyperdreams: Damien Broderick's Space/Time Fiction.* P.O. Box 170 New Lambton, Australia: Nimrod Publications, 1998.
Broderick, Damien. *The Black Grail.* Melbourne: Mandarin, 1990.
———. *Sorcerer's World.* New York: Signet, 1970.
Chambers Dictionary of Foreign Words and Phrases.
Clute, John and Peter Nicholls. *The Science Fiction Encyclopedia.* New York: St. Martin's Press, 1993.
Fogg, Martyn J. *Terraforming: Engineering Planetary Environments.* Warrendale, Pennsylvania: Society of Automotive Engineers, Inc., 1995.
Oxford English Dictionary.
Oxford Russian Dictionary.
Sturluson, Snorri (trans. Jean I. Young). *The Prose Edda.* Berkeley: UC Press, 1973.
Temianka, Dan. *The Jack Vance Lexicon.* San Bernardino, California: The Borgo Press, 1995.
Vance, Jack. *Rhialto the Marvellous.* New York: Baen, 1985.

SF ROCK: BOWIE AND NUMAN

Science Fiction was very good to David Bowie. His first big hit, "Space Oddity" (1969) describes an astronaut who succumbs to a mind-expanding rapture of outer space while in his first orbit. It was inspired by the "journey into the monolith" trip near the end of Kubrick's epic movie *2001: A Space Odyssey* (1968), and its release was delayed so the song would arrive just in time for the first Moon landings. The single rocketed to #5 in the UK charts (1969), but this was not enough to get the album on the charts.

Bowie was no stranger to science fiction, and a few of his earlier songs have science fiction themes. "We Are Hungry Men" (1967) depicts a breathless scientist, a self-proclaimed messiah, who has just come up with a new technological solution to chronic overpopulation—only to find that the crowd he is talking to has come up with the old solution of cannibalism. "Cygnet Committee" (1969) tells of a cultural revolution that starts off with sweetness and light but then turns ugly, ending with the revolution's "love machines" killing civilians in the streets. "Wild Eyed Boy from Freecloud" (1969), which first appeared as the B-side of the "Space Oddity" single, is a fantasy vignette about a strange boy, a "missionary mystic of peace/love," whom the unsympathetic mountain villagers try to hang as a witch (in a surprisingly brutal twist, the mountain sends an avalanche to kill them and save his boy).

After the success of "Space Oddity," Bowie dabbled a bit more, along the same lines, with a couple more songs. "Saviour

Machine" (1970) returns to Kubrick's *Space Odyssey*, this time for the computer HAL, who is installed as the titular dingus to rule a golden age of Earth—for a while, at least, until the machine becomes bored with the god-like power it has and turns to more Satanic pursuits. "The Supermen" (1970) is a Lovecraftian story of bright Atlantean ubermench and their dark end.

Bowie's early albums reveal a spectrum of musical styles including folk, music hall, psychedelia, and a bit of heavy metal. Science Fiction had shown results, and he reinvested heavily, aiming squarely at pop rock. The resulting masterpiece, *The Rise and Fall of Ziggy Stardust and the Spiders from Mars* (1972), is a concept album about a Martian with a message of peace and love, a popular messiah who is unfortunately destroyed by his own excesses. The story itself is told through several different viewpoint characters: the album begins with a young man's reaction to the somber newscast declaring that Earth will soon die of an unspecified, unstoppable eco-disaster ("Five Years"); a few songs later, two kids hear a strange song on the radio, the first sign of the coming extraterrestrial and his message of hope ("Starman"); two songs after that, Ziggy arrives in all his androgynous glory, concert footage narrated by a fan ("Lady Stardust"); then Ziggy himself sings his dream of being a British pop rock star ("Star"); one pop hit later comes the title track, in which Ziggy's manager summarizes Ziggy's brief career as having begun with bright hope and ended in dark corruption ("Ziggy Stardust"); and the album ends with a narrator addressing a Ziggy who wanders the streets like a real or figurative ghost, meeting a hint of hope/redemption at the very end ("Rock 'n' Roll Suicide").

So it is all a reworking of the messianic heroes in "Wild Eyed Boy" and "Hungry Men" into the meteoric rise and fall of a rock star ("when the kids had killed the man I had to break up the band" as the title song goes), but the eleven tracks include several catchy pop tunes that became hits. Beyond the overall concept, the science fiction content is relatively light, with a toss off reference to the "droogs" of Kubrick's *A Clockwork Orange* (1971) in the song "Hang on to Yourself." This album, Bowie's fifth in six years, made him a true pop star, reaching #5 (UK) and #75 (US), and the character of Ziggy Stardust proved to be highly marketable.

Bowie's next album, *Aladdin Sane* (1973), has less science fiction content than *Ziggy Stardust*. The album's main theme is one of social collapse, which was hardly confined to genre at the time. The song "Drive-In Saturday" is the most science-fictional, portraying a dissipated future where the dwindling population watches old porn movies to relearn biological reproduction techniques. These film showings are perhaps sponsored by extraterrestrials "the strange ones in the domes"—like zookeepers trying to get their captive pandas to mate by showing them videos of pandas mating in the wild. The album hit #1 (UK) and #17 (US).

But Bowie had not yet given up on genre. In fact, he was investing even more heavily in it, trying to incorporate the biggest established works he could.

Diamond Dogs (1974) is a concept album about a post-apocalyptic world, blending Orwell's *1984* (1949) with Bowie's gender-bending glam rock. Bowie had wanted to make a rock musical version of *1984*, but the Orwell estate denied him permission. The Orwell content of *Diamond Dogs* is still rather high, as evidenced by such songs as "Big Brother," "1984," and "We Are the Dead" (the famous line uttered by Winston Smith just before being captured by the Thought Police). "Future Legend" opens the album, painting the post-apocalypse landscape in broad strokes of vivid color in a few spoken lines: "And in the death, as the last few corpses lay rotting on the slimy thoroughfare," followed by "red mutant eyes gaze down on Hunger City," and ending with the shouted lines, "This ain't rock and roll. This is genocide!"

The story, such as it is, seems to be about a Party member who is gay—whether this is a scandalous secret or a prerequisite for Party membership is unclear. This "Winston Smith" surrogate is, despite his gay lifestyle, stunted and dead inside, nearly suicidal. But then he meets a life-reviving "Julia," a self-professed rebel, who is in this case a cross-dressing, glam-rocking teenage boy prostitute. (The pedophilic details are almost cringe-worthy:

"I'm glad that you're older than me, it makes me feel important and free" ("Sweet Thing").) From there on, Orwell's basic story follows its course: the happy lovers are separated and broken so that all love flows from the individual to the State.

Diamond Dogs hit #1 (UK) and #5 (US), going Gold the same year.

After completing this trilogy of sorts, Bowie abandoned science fiction in his music for the rest of the decade. A later album, *Low* (1977), was largely electronic music with a certain science-fictional texture, but none of the content. During the same period Bowie starred in Nicolas Roeg's science fiction movie *The Man Who Fell to Earth* (1976), his casting based largely on the strength of Ziggy's marketability. With this transition to film in mind, perhaps a better way to put it would be to say that science fiction enveloped Bowie for the movie after he so successfully used science fiction as a tool for his music.

If there is a real market for something, then it can be successfully imitated. The rise of Gary Numan shows the continuing marketability of science fiction rock in the late 1970s, after Bowie had left science fiction music behind.

Numan's early punk-influenced tunes, released in 1978, failed to make the charts, but the science fiction themes on debut album *Tubeway Army* (1978) got enough attention for the album to sell out. The opening track "Listen to the Sirens" directly references Philip K. Dick's novel *Flow My Tears, The Policeman Said* (1974) in its first line: "'Flow My Tears,' the new police song." Another song, "Steel and You," begins Numan's highly profitable allusions to androids. "My Love is a Liquid" has the line "Do you know that friends come in boxes?" an allusion to Michael G. Coney's novel *Friends Come in Boxes* (1973), a text Numan would source again more deeply.

The sound of the album *Tubeway Army* is rather close to the bright pop rock of Bowie's *Ziggy Stardust*, substituting post-punk details for the thoroughly defunct glam rock. But Bowie had moved on in the six years since 1972, and Numan seems to have followed his lead, such that his next album was a melding of Bowie '72 science fictional content and Bowie '77 electronic music form. On the science fiction content front, Numan was clearly doing his homework, and doing it thoroughly: where Bowie alluded to big names like Kubrick and Orwell, Numan was going for the lesser-known but more authentic works of PKD and Coney.

Replicas (April 1979) is a concept album heavily influenced by both PKD's novel *Do Androids Dream of Electric Sheep?* (1968) and Michael G. Coney's *Friends Come in Boxes* (1973). PKD's most famous novel is about a bounty hunter who retires rogue androids on a dying Earth—these androids, murderous escaped slaves, are like pod-people in that they take the places of existing humans and can only be discovered through an empathy test. Once discovered, the androids are killed. Coney's novel is also about androids, but in this case they are created in order to house the brains of deceased humans—brains that are kept alive in black boxes, entities known as "friends." Coney's androids live and care for "friends," knowing that their own personalities will be destroyed so the friends can inhabit their bodies.

Numan knits these two different texts together by positing "gray men" (authority figures decked out in matching gray overcoats and hats) who administer tests to determine who is real and who is not. "Friends" are electric robot companions that still cause sadness to humans when they break down: "You know, I hate to ask, but are friends electric? Mine's burned out and now I've no one to love." "Machmen" (which sounds like "mock men") are human/machine hybrids, being robots with outer layers of human flesh. To this he adds wandering extraterrestrials and robots that go on murderous rampages, not unlike Bowie's "strange ones in the domes" and "love machines," respectively.

Replicas is not so much a story as it is a description of a mental condition and a nightmarish place. The protagonists are young men who have memory problems, powerless individuals who are preyed upon by pedophilic men and machines alike. Their memory problems include false memories ("I was in a car crash, or was it the war, but I've never been quite the same. Little white lies like 'I was there'" ("Down in the Park")), self-identity dissonance ("I couldn't recognize my photograph" ("Me! I Disconnect from You")), and more general amnesia ("Yellowed newspapers tell the story of someone. 'Do you know this man?'" ("The Machman"); "And just for a second I thought I remembered you" ("Are 'Friends' Electric?"); "And the light fades out and I wonder what I'm doing in a room like this?" All of this recalls the sort of trauma often associated with UFO abductees.

The place is a wild, gloomy city, rather a lot like the Interzone of William Burroughs crossed with The Village of Patrick McGoohan's TV series "The Prisoner" (1967–68). It is centered on The Park, a landscaped arena where humans (perhaps those who fail the test given by the gray men) are hunted by Machmen and robots, a gory spectacle sport best viewed from the safety of the overlooking restaurant Zom-Zom's.

As in the case of Bowie's work in *Diamond Dogs*, there is cringe-worthy pedophilic content. Where Bowie's boy hustler is gritty and grimy, yet still romantic and full of street-power, Numan's analog is a powerless victim: "the driver wants to touch me . . . I try to back away but he's so strong I just can't move. Maybe I don't want to anyway" ("It Must Have Been Years"); "I could feel his mind decaying only inches away from me" ("Me! I Disconnect from You"); "I saw him turn on like a machine in the park, saying 'Please come with me.' You know you've been there before" ("The Machman"). It is as if the questionable sentiment of 1962's "Go Away Little Girl" had been replaced in the late 1970s with an unambiguous *Hold Still Little Boy*.

The sound of *Replicas* is techno rock, a bridge between the rock of *Tubeway Army* and the techno pop of *The Pleasure Principle* (1979). *Replicas* hit the right notes to capture #1 (UK) in 1979. While the title seems like a sly acknowledgement of being a "copy" (of Bowie), it eerily predicts the term "replicants" used for androids in the movie version of *Do Androids Dream of Electric*

Sheep? (Ridley Scott's *Blade Runner* (1982)). Furthermore, while the accomplished electronic music artist Vangelis composed the soundtrack for *Blade Runner*, still it sounds more like Numan than earlier Vangelis work, and sounds nothing like Bowie's electronica.

Numan followed with a second album that year, *The Pleasure Principle* (September 1979). This is a techno pop record, a light version, and guitar free. There is no unifying science fiction theme, just a scattering of androids, robots, and engineers. Still, the bouncy single "Cars," about a Ballardian sort of driver more at home in his vehicle than in his house, became Numan's biggest hit, driving up to #1 (UK), #10 (US, 1980), and charting worldwide. With all this going on, *Tubeway Army* was re-issued and made it to #14 (UK). What a year for Gary Numan, with three of his albums charting, and two of them striking #1! And what a year for science fiction Rock!

SF HERESIES #1 & #2

Number 1: Martian War Tripod Locomotion

How do those heavy assault craft of H. G. Wells's *The War of the Worlds* really move, anyhow?

John Christopher's White Mountains series, clearly an homage to Wells, has the alien Masters walk their three-legged-walk with a whirling gait. This is like "walking" a drawing compass by using its points as alternating steps, drawing a sequence of intersecting half-circles, but with three points instead of only two.

Larry Niven's Puppeteers are three legged aliens, and when they get moving fast it is a gallop with the two front in tandem and the rear leg pushing off, or kicking the pursuing party.

My theory is that the Martian tripod walks on two legs. The third leg is carried like a tail.

Well then, you say, why bother having three legs at all? Why not have Martian bipods?

Two reasons: turning radius and recoil due to heavy weapons.

A bipod turning to move 60 degrees off of the current line of movement would have to pivot all that way, whereas a tripod walking bipedally merely changes its tail into a leg, converts the now trailing leg into a tail, and moves in the new direction. When it has advanced to the point at which it wants to fire, the tail is lowered for greater stability and the heat ray gun is activated.

Tripods have no fixed "flanks," they have alternating flanks, just as they have no fixed "front." Their ability to change course without pivoting means that they move somewhat more like helicopter gunships than tanks (tanks are rather bipedal, come to think of it). They would move in strange diagonal lines, almost like the Bishops in chess.

Number 2: Big Brother Is Australian

Everybody seems to think that Orwell's Big Brother is American, that the superstate of Oceania in *Nineteen Eighty-Four* represents an American-dominated Free World.

I firmly disagree.

It seems to me that what I am about to outline should be in Cliff's Notes, yet it is not. Nor is it in the interesting *1984 Revisited* (edited by Irving Howe, published in 1983).

Start with the names of the superstates: Eastasia, Eurasia, and Oceania. Everyone agrees that the first two are geographical terms, but for some odd reason everyone shies away from the fact that the third one is, too! A dictionary will tell you, "Oceania: Islands of the central, West, and South Pacific Ocean, usually including Australia and New Zealand." It seems that among the geography-deniers there is some sense that since Oceania is a sea-power, then the name Oceania is applied purely for the "Ocean" in its name.

Next take a look at the "future history" of the novel. People seem to think that the novel depicts a world where something like WWII has been going on for nearly 40 years. Well yes, kind of, but there was an atomic war that lasted for most of the 1950s, a war fought between Oceania and Eurasia, and at the end of this period the third superstate, Eastasia, emerged. Since we know that Eastasia includes Japan and Korea, we can glimpse an alternate history where Oceanian (U.S.) forces were driven from Korea in the early '50s (i.e., losing what was to be the Korean War) and from Japan soon thereafter. (Vietnam lies within the zone of perpetual conflict in the world of *1984*, and as such is not a permanent possession of any superstate.) And as Eurasia represents a Russian takeover of all of continental Europe, the U.S. forces were early on swept from there as well (i.e., there was no containment of Russian expansion).

Orwell clearly felt that the Cold War between the U.S. and

the Soviet Union would soon erupt into nuclear war. A United States of America that had endured ten years of atomic war on its own soil would not be in very good shape, to put it mildly. The place should be in worse condition than Europe after World War II, with greater lingering effects due to radiation. We would expect that all the initial military and industrial targets have been nuked, and the farmlands have been poisoned with fallout (although the information on fallout in 1948 was pretty sketchy). For this reason it seems likely that headquarters would relocate to somewhere else, and Australia seems like a good spot (see Shute's *On the Beach* for a well-known later example of Australia as last refuge from nuclear warfare).

Finally, a look at the zone of conflict, that "rough quadrilateral with its corners at Tangier, Brazzaville, Darwin, and Hong Kong" containing the people and resources that change ownership among the three superstates in their perpetual battles for materials (as opposed to the constant warfare in the Arctic Circle, which must be more a battle of strategic positioning). The United States is rather far away from the material zone, and sea lanes pass through the contested area of the Pacific Ocean, but Australia is right there on the edge of the action, making core areas (say France, China, and Australia) all within range of easy access and easy utility.

I think that Orwell was looking around at the "American-occupied" United Kingdom of World War II and he was thinking that the same thing would happen to America. So the Oceania of *Nineteen Eighty-Four* has a battered American hegemony which is dead but does not yet know it, braced up and being supplanted by Australians (just as the British Empire had been replaced by American hegemony by 1948).

Whether the Americans fled to Australia as a "New Washington" in the manner that the Roman leadership left Rome for Constantine's New Rome is a moot point. In the same "Yankophobic" vein, I think that Orwell's celebrated "Newspeak" is less related to William Barnes and the Pure English movement and more a poke at American spelling taking over the Anglophonic world.

TOYNBEE AND SF: ASIMOV AND DE CAMP

The British historian Arnold J. Toynbee (1889–1975) had a powerful influence on American science fiction in the formative 1940s. Before examining the genre influence, a brief look at his massive work, *A Study in History*, is in order.

The first six volumes of *A Study in History* were published before World War Two and became a best seller after the war. (He later wrote an additional six volumes, published from 1954 to 1961, for a total of twelve volumes.) Toynbee's goal was to transform history from an Art into a Science by tracing universal or "metahistorical" patterns discernable in all civilizations. His view was that all civilizations rise, decay, and collapse in the same basic steps.

In his books, Toynbee finds the unit of scale for historical study to be the civilization, rather than the smaller units of either the ethnic group or the nation. According to Toynbee, civilizations arise in a core area of challenging geography, expand to adjacent areas during a Growth Stage, and then face a fratricidal War Stage. This conflict is ultimately resolved through the establishment of a Universal State, and when this breaks down there comes the Interregnum, a stage that ends in one of two ways: either the civilization will live by restoring its Universal State, or it will die.

Thus, for example, rather than a "Roman Civilization," Toynbee sees the Roman Republic as the leading edge of Hellenic Civilization during its late Growth Stage; the same Republic was the final victor in the Hellenic War Stage (a series of conflicts beginning with the Peloponnesian War, continuing through the conquests of Alexander, and ending with the Roman Civil Wars); and the Roman Empire was the Hellenic Universal State. At its Interregnum, Hellenic Civilization broke into three geographical chunks: the core, centered on Constantinople; the old frontier, centered on Rome; and the new frontier, centered on northern France. This arrangement led to a tug of war between the Byzantine Empire, the Church of Rome, and the Frankish kingdom. Toynbee argues that this challenge might have been won in AD 800 by Charlemagne, as a strongman from the new frontier who restores the Universal State. Charlemagne failed, however, which allowed Hellenic Civilization to die and Western Civilization to arise as its daughter.

In addition to examining full-fledged civilizations, Toynbee also writes about "abortive civilizations" that were snuffed out in their infancy. One example is the Far Western Christian Civilization, centered on Ireland's Celtic Church, an embryonic civilization that was crippled at the Synod of Whitby in 664 and subsequently destroyed by Vikings in later centuries. Scandinavian Civilization, centered on Iceland, was itself another abortive one, first compromised by adopting Frankish culture at Normandy in 910, and ultimately voted out of existence in AD 1000 when Iceland adopted Roman Christianity.

Toynbee is very clear in illustrating that not all of history is determined in the clash of hard power on the battlefield. There are plenty of examples of soft power versus soft power, such as the case at Whitby in 664 where the Church of Rome won against the Celtic Church. And the hard power of the Vikings fell to the soft power of Western Civilization, first in Normandy and finally in Iceland.

Toynbee says that there are no inherent racial or ethnic qualities — all humans are the same, shaped only by the challenges (both physical and social) they face and the responses they make. Thus Toynbee's famous pattern of "Challenge and Response." When a civilization faces a challenge that it cannot respond to, it suffers a crisis. Such crises mark the transitions from one stage to another—from Growth to War, from War to Universal State, and from Universal State to Interregnum. So it seems deterministic, yet it allows for cultural free will, cultural choices, and cultural consequences.

This concludes the Toybee briefing. Now onward to Toynbee's deep influence upon science fiction in the 1940s.

Asimov's Galactic Empire

> *The empire remains the favorite symbol of the large state, and it has taken over the imagination of the science fiction world.... For this, I myself am largely responsible.... It was my Foundation series...that set the fashion. (Asimov, Introduction to Intergalactic Empires, 9)*

Isaac Asimov's Foundation stories (1942 to 1951) had a profound impact on the genre. In the prologue, a visionary scientist, a Psychohistorian, discovers that the galactic empire will soon fall into a dark age lasting 30,000 years. Against this coming disaster he devises a plan, setting up the titular Foundation on a distant world in such an ingenious way as to ensure that the coming historical forces will propel it to restore the empire in a mere 1000 years. The stories tell the saga of the empire's decline and the rebuilding efforts of the Foundation.

The initial Foundation stories seem to be an experiment in working out Toynbee's theory on a galactic scale. Asimov's galaxy has no intelligent life other than humanity, thus there are no alien cycles to factor in, and with an FTL system that puts the entire galaxy within easy reach, the human experience in space will be quite a lot like that on Earth, where location (physical, geographical) and the cultural responses made at each challenge are the determinants (since all humans are equally "plastic"). Not the least is the fact that Asimov's "Psychohistory," a science of history such that a master can predict future events based upon initial geography and cycles of "challenge and response," seems like a simple extension of Toynbee's metahistory.

Initially the location and physical condition of planet Terminus is paramount. It is a small, barren, worthless world at the edge of the galaxy, populated only by the Encyclopedists, a band of scholars working to preserve the cultural heritage of their galactic civilization. Thus they are analogous to monks in Ireland, transplanted to Iceland, but instead of being a religious brotherhood working to evolve the new church, they are a secular group working to preserve knowledge and restore the Roman Empire.

So in essence, Asimov is positing an alternate history about the fall of the Roman Empire and the rise of a Second Roman Empire after a greatly shortened medieval period. The Psychohistorian's Plan would reduce the time between the sack of Rome (AD 409) and the Renaissance (1400). Asimov's capital world Trantor is a version of Rome, and Terminus is an Icelandic Ultima Thule. To follow the historical models above, Asimov will have someone like Charlemagne and his paladins reestablishing the empire circa 800 as a Holy Roman Empire. So the resulting renaissance will be a much more literal one: a resurrection.

The stories seem to bear this out. In "The Encyclopedists," the Foundation faces a physical challenge in the lack of metal on their world and the hard power belligerence of four neo-barbarian planets nearby. They respond by successfully playing each off the other. In "The Mayors," the Foundation uses its technological edge to create an artificial religion called Scientism to exert soft-power control over its neighbors, in the same way that Irish monks might have converted the Vikings to Celtic Christianity.

But however much it seems to be inspired by Toynbee, the author in his autobiography begs to differ: "There are some people who, upon reading my Foundation series, are sure that it was influenced basically by Toynbee ... The first four stories were written before I had read Toynbee" (*In Memory Yet Green*, p. 400).

This is very interesting. It calls for a detailed look at the genesis of the Foundation series.

Asimov writes (*In Memory Yet Green*, p. 311) that on August 1,

1941, he was a young man (21 years old) sitting on a train on the way to see magazine editor John W. Campbell to talk about his next story idea, but the problem was he actually had no idea yet. So he opened his book at random and saw a picture that made him think of medieval times, the fall of civilization and the interregnum. Which reminded him of Gibbon's *The Decline and Fall of the Roman Empire* (which he had read twice).

With this, he went to Campbell and they hashed out the Foundation, and Psychohistory, and then Asimov wrote "The Encyclopedists" (the second story in the final sequence published as the book *Foundation*). The story proved popular, so he tried to write a sequel, but it proved too difficult until he had a meeting with his friend Fredrick Pohl:

> *His suggestions were excellent ones, but what they were, I don't remember ... In any case, I rushed home, began work again, and found the story moving easily. Without Pohl I don't know if I could have managed, and then what would have happened to the Foundation series? (319)*

The resulting story, "The Mayors," was also popular, and Asimov wrote two more without further difficulty. These four stories cemented his career.

Because of all these threads, I have a suspicion that young Asimov, the Gibbonist, found himself somehow the author of a Toynbee-derived experiment: he had been directed into this role by subtle agents of Toynbee. John W. Campbell obviously had a strong hand in shaping the series out of nearly nothing, but was he a fan of Toynbee? It seems quite plausible. Then there is Pohl and the mysterious advice he gave: Was he a Toynbeean? In any event, all the fans that read the Foundation stories with such gusto were Toynbeeans, whether they knew it or not.

After the first four Foundation stories (1942–1944), the textual evolution of the remaining five becomes tricky. Asimov notes in his autobiography how his friend L. Sprague de Camp loaned his six volumes of Toynbee to Asimov in the spring of 1944:

> *After the war [ended in 1945], Toynbee went through a period of great, though temporary, popularity. Sprague, however, was an admirer long before the rest of the world caught on. (p. 400)*

Asimov read Toynbee and was enthused for a while, enough so that the next Foundation story was consciously modeled on Toynbee. This story, "The General," is pretty clearly a retelling of Belisarius, the Byzantine military man who retook Italy and Sicily for the East Roman Empire. (The character's name is "Bel Riose.") So the Foundation time line is at that point equivalent to our AD 535.

But then Asimov's enthusiasm for Toynbee evaporated. When he wrote the next story in the sequence, Asimov began a series of radical breaks with the original concept of Foundation, to the point that it starts to look as though he meant to destroy it. Granted, Asimov may have felt that he had painted himself (or "had been painted") into a corner. He was running out of tricks in playing the free will vs. determinism game that the scenario might seem to require.

So Asimov introduced a wild card, the Mule (purportedly based on the 14th century Mongol warlord Timur the Lame, but he seems much more like the 7th century Arab Prophet Mohammed), playing perhaps on Campbell's interest in psionic mutant powers. Here was something that the Psychohistorian could not have predicted! Then Asimov brought in the Second Foundation, which is basically an Illuminati group that uses direct action to correct things whenever the predicted "history" starts to "go wrong." Thus Psychohistory itself is something of a sham, a weird messianic science-religion of "chosen people" that is really all being shaped by hidden human conspirators.

In a strange way, it almost seems as though Asimov was a Gibbonite acting out against the Toynbeean influencers and the Toynbeean fanbase. He was pushing back against the "mind control" that they had used on him in a manner similar to the way that the Second Foundation's psionic powers are used to shape minds.

The autobiography shows that Campbell, Pohl, and de Camp guided Asimov's writing of the Foundation series at different periods. Of the three, de Camp is identified as being a Toynbee fan. This clue leads us to examine the work of de Camp for influence of Toynbee.

De Camp's Alternate Histories

A few years before Asimov created the galactic empire subgenre, his friend L. Sprague de Camp had written two seminal novels that effectively launched the alternate history subgenre as we know it today: *Lest Darkness Fall* (1939) and *Wheels of If* (1940). Both novels show a strong influence of Toynbee's *A Study of History*.

Lest Darkness Fall is very much like Twain's *A Connecticut Yankee in King Arthur's Court* (1889). In both novels a modern man is transported through time into the distant past where he tries to improve things with modern devices. De Camp's hero winds up in the Rome of AD 535, when it is the capital of an Ostrogothic kingdom, just in time to face General Belisarius's attempt to reconquer Italy for Byzantium (AD 535 to 540).

This is an interesting moment in history because Rome had already been sacked (twice!) and the last emperor of the West Roman Empire had been deposed about sixty years before. By most accounts, the "darkness" had already fallen. But Toynbee, writing about the beginning of the dark ages in the West Roman Empire, asserts,

> It is perhaps not so readily recognized that the same fate overtook the original Roman Empire in the East, as well, before the Dark Ages were over. Its dissolution may be equated with the end of the strenuous and disastrous reign of Justinian in AD 565. There followed in the East a century-and-a-half of interregnum ... in which the remains of a

dead society were swept away and the foundations of a successor were laid. (I, 369–70)

So, in Toynbee's view, de Camp's hero Padway has arrived at a critical juncture: after the fall of Rome but before the end of the East Roman Empire. Padway's knowledge of history gives him the prophetic power of a psychohistorian, and his flood of new tools and ideas put him in a good position to be the leader of a new frontier who will restore the Universal State of Hellenic Civilization.

In this manner it seems that de Camp, through a close reading of Toynbee, had concluded that Charlemagne's failure to restore Hellenic Civilization's Universal State in AD 800 was due to the fact that the East Roman Empire had already fallen in AD 565. Thus his hero Padway in 535 has thirty years to succeed where Charlemagne failed.

De Camp's next novel, *Wheels of If* (1940), opened up the wild nature of an altered timeline. Once again a modern man is cast into a strange world, but in this case it is an alternate 1940 where the timeline is radically different: a New York City called "New Belfast" in a nation called Vinland, an Irish-Anglo-Scandinavian country where the oppressed minority is the American Indian. The key turning points warping this timeline from our own are the Synod of Whitby (AD 664) where England went to the Celtic Church, which then rapidly spread to Scandinavia, and the Battle of Tours (AD 732), where the Arabs defeated the Franks. Then a Viking explorer discovered North America in 989, so the Christianized Vikings went colonizing Vinland in the 11th century rather than crusading in the Middle East. In this North America, the pressing social issue is one of American Indian Rights, and a potential war is brewing between the white states of the East and the red states of the Great Plains. That is to say, de Camp posits a type of Civil Rights Movement as a precursor to a sort of War Between the States.

It seems wildly inventive, and it is, yet I believe the seeds can be found in Toynbee's work. The focus on the Synod of Whitby as a key turning point seems straight out of Toynbee, and the

Celtic Church's use of soft power against Scandinavia also fits. De Camp thus rescues two abortive civilizations by having them fuse together into one, with the soft power of the Celtic Church combined with the hard power of the Vikings. But there is more, as revealed by this passage from Toynbee in discussing the history of Christianity in England and the fallout of Whitby:

> *The first chapter is the peaceful conversion of the English by a band of Roman missionaries, but this is followed by the coercion of the Far Western Christians by a series of turns of the screw which began with the decision of the Synod of Whitby in AD 664 and culminated in the armed invasion of Ireland by Henry II of England, with Papal approval, in 1171. Nor is this the end of the story. Habits of 'frightfulness' acquired by the English in their prolonged aggression against the remnants of the Celtic Fringe in the Highlands of Scotland and the bogs of Ireland, were carried across the Atlantic and practiced at the expense of the North American Indians. (473)*

Toynbee states that if the Synod of Whitby had gone the other way, then the English would not have been so savage with the American Indians. This seems to fit perfectly with de Camp's Vinland.

Wheels of If is chock full of wonderment, from alternate technology marvels like pneumatic machineguns and steam-turbined airplanes, to anthropological details on nudism taboos. One element that really shines is de Camp's way of showing an English language where words are still sounded out the way they are spelled. So knight is "knick," right is "rick," frightful is "frickful," thought is "thock," and vehicles are "wains" of various types: cars are "wains," buses are "folkwains," trucks are "goodwains," and airplanes are "airwains." (A dictionary is a "Wördbuk.") The language is more like Middle English, clearly signaling the lack of a Norman Invasion (AD 1066) in this timeline, but there is also a strong cue from Toynbee. In an anecdote about "language purity" movements applied to English, Toynbee writes:

> *Some thirty years ago, one calling himself 'C. L. D.' published a Word-Book of the English Tongue for the guidance of those who long 'to shake off the Norman yoke' which lies so heavy on our speech.... Following 'C. L. D.' we should call a peramulator a childwain and an omnibus a folkwain; and these might be improvements. But when he seeks to get rid of resident aliens whose domicile is of more ancient date he is less happy. When he proposes to replace 'disapprove' by 'hiss,' 'boo' or 'hoot' he hardly hits the nail on the head and he hits it much too hard; and 'redecraft,' 'backjaw' and 'outganger' are unconvincing substitutes for 'logic,' 'retort' and 'emigrant.' (581)*

It seems likely that in addition to key elements of the altered timeline being inspired by Toynbee, so too were the novel's linguistic flourishes.

By this evidence it seems clear that Toynbee had a profound influence on science fiction in the 1940s by inspiring works that are not only considered classics but also considered the starting points of well-defined subgenres. Even though Asimov was a Gibbonite who ultimately rejected Toynbee, still he somehow managed to establish his career writing Toynbee stories. De Camp, on the other hand, was a Toynbee fan who carefully studied the source material and consciously incorporated many surprising details.

Bibliography

Asimov, Isaac. *In Memory Yet Green*. New York: Doubleday & Co, Inc., 1979.

Asimov, Isaac and Martin H. Greenberg and Charles G. Waugh (editors). *Intergalactic Empires*. New York: New American Library, 1983.

de Camp, L. Sprague. *Lest Darkness Fall.* New York: Ballantine Books, 1974.

———. *The Virgin & The Wheels* (omnibus edition of *The Virgin of Zesh* and *The Wheels of If*). New York: Popular Library, 1976.

Toynbee, Arnold J. *A Study in History (abridged, two-volume version).*

New York: Dell Publishing, 1965.

SF HERESY #3

Number 3: Vinge's "Singularity" As Western Civ's Empire Or Universal Church

Inspired by reading Damien Broderick's *The Spike* (2001), which examines the trending phenomenon popularized in genre by Vernor Vinge as the technological "Singularity," an event of such magnitude as to sunder something or other. Broderick terms this event "the Spike," and Vernor Vinge says it will come sometime between 2030 and 2100.

Plus I've read all the Vinge fiction, enthusiastically. (But it is kind of funny that Vinge, for having put the Spike on the map, hasn't really written much about it at all. It is in a lot of things he has written, but always in the background. Which makes it perfect for readers to glom onto: if he just came out and gave a straight account in fictional form, many readers might just say, "Yeah, but that's stupid." By saying little, he allows readers to fill in the blanks to their own hearts delight. In the end it might be pretty much like Cordwainer Smith's huge future history; oceanic seeming, but not really there as much as one is led to believe.)

Since I have too much Toynbee on the brain, as you may recall (in fact my Toynbee kick started with reading the Barnes pamphlet *How to Build a Future*), I also had a sort of Toynbeean analysis going on at the same time as I was reading *The Spike*.

First point being that Western Civ is technocentric, and as such is relatively rare among civilizations (around 4%, using Toynbee's figures, but I'm sure he would say that is an upper range). (So sf would seem to have a very special place for Western Civilization: practically a sacred text/dialogue!)

Second point being that civilizations are not immortal, and have lifespans averaging 2000 years, divided into four stages: Growth, War, Universal State, and Universal Church. Western Civ has been in the War stage, on the threshold of a Universal State, for hundreds of years now, but technically War is still a period of growth (technology, in our sense, since we are technocentric). The Universal State is a period where growth is halted (in our case it would be technology). Note that the "warring" is internal to the civilization, not external (Spain trying to unify Europe; France trying it; Germany trying). By Toynbee's model, the War stage cannot last forever, in fact, cannot drag out much longer than it has already: if a civilization's warring elements overtax themselves by the effort the entire civilization will be overrun by an external civilization and/or barbarians.

In this light, the Spike itself might be anticipation of the Universal State (point where growth ends abruptly; one cannot "see beyond it" because nothing new happens and the dominant attitude becomes "all things have been discovered") and/or the Universal Church (the final stage where the civilization's focus is transformed into a higher religion: again, in our case this means a "world religion" based upon technology, i.e., a church of sf). So the range of dates for the Spike seem to match Toynbee's sense of stages (I intuit).

Not to get mystical about it, but more like the central memes of the civilization just run out of gas, having expressed themselves though x number of generations, through x cycles of thesis, antithesis, synthesis. People stop having children; the civilization "turns inward" (as John Barnes puts it in his piece "How to Build a Future"). Nothing lasts forever: in youth, summer seems endless; until the bubble bursts, it seems as if the trend (dot com; high tech stocks; post industrial economy) will last forever; and so on.

It isn't that technological advance reaches a real end, it just reaches a perceived end. It is a very "millennial" feeling. The franchise is no longer offered to members outside the civilization, who, being thus locked out, become true "barbarians." All the traits of a Universal State quickly rise up in a predictable way.

The kicker: if Western Civ cannot grab the Promethean sfnal goodies on this run, then humanity will have to wait for another technocentric civ to try it ... a wait of a few millennium, at least, since a technocentric civ cannot be born of a technocentric civ (daughter civs are always different in respects like this). All those "post-apocalyptic" scenarios of a post-technological world are thus validated, not by the radioactive wastelands or the hordes of mutants, nor even the eco-ruin and the lack of easy materials to work with, but by the fact that the civilization to come after Western Civ will, by definition, be one that is not technocentric.

Maybe the collective unconscious has a vague awareness of the civilization's age and stage?

The Apocalypse of John was written circa AD 95. The Toynbee context is that Hellenic Civilization was in its Universal State period, centered on Rome. The persecutions of Christians was pretty terrible and it was to continue for a few centuries. From this terrible background springs the Apocalypse, a work that is famous for its, well, apocalyptic vision, but I would like to distinguish now between the "mundane" and the "transcendent" apocalypses. The transcendent apocalypse does not seem to have happened just yet, and has been "just around the corner" for quite some time. But the mundane apocalypse really did happen, and rather quickly, too.

Apocalypse of John: AD 95
Milan Edict of Toleration (end of persecution): AD 313
Christianity State Religion: AD 391
End of Hellenic Civilization: AD 476

Toynbee says that when Christianity became the state religion, Hellenic Civilization had shifted from the Universal State into the Universal Church, the final stage for nearly all civilizations. Or to put it another way, in AD 391 Rome became the New Jerusalem, and this lasted for less than a hundred years, at which point "the world ended"—the world in this case being Hellenic Civilization.

WES ANDERSON AND ERB

Wes Anderson, the director/writer of eight feature films including *The Grand Budapest Hotel* (2014), *Moonrise Kingdom* (2012), *The Royal Tenenbaums* (2001), and so on, is said to be the great-grandson of Edgar Rice Burroughs. One can find this claim repeated on the Internet in countless blogs, as well as on such curated sites as Wikipedia (entries on "Edgar Rice Burroughs" and "Wes Anderson") and IMDB (entry for "Edgar Rice Burroughs"). The first mention of this lineage seems to be from Jeffrey Wells in a *Los Angeles Times* article "Lost in Filmland?" (Nov 7, 1993), where, in the third to the last paragraph, it states that Wes Anderson is "descended from literary royalty (he's the great-grandson of Edgar Rice Burroughs)."

While this statement of a bloodline linking Wes to ERB has been floating around for over 21 years, it is apparently never backed up with any further substance. What little we know about the director's lineage is that his full name is Wesley Wales Anderson, and we have the names of the nuclear family he grew up in: father Melver Anderson; mother Texas Ann; brothers Mel and Eric Chase.

Since Wes does not have the surname Burroughs, we somewhat rashly suppose the ERB connection to be on his mother's side; and lo, said mother's maiden name was, in fact, Burroughs. "Texas Ann" certainly sounds like the name of an ERB heroine (perhaps from one of the several Westerns he wrote), and the fact that Texas Ann Anderson was an archeologist at one time further adds to the ERB-quality of adventure-in-a-name.

On the other hand, the descendents of ERB are fairly well documented (for example, the premiere of movie *John Carter* was attended by great-granddaughters Dejah Burroughs and her sister Llana Jane Burroughs, both named after ERB heroines). Well, I first thought the family lines were documented and clear, but in delving deeper I found some instances of second marriages, adoptions, and things of that sort. Such that Texas Ann might be descended from ERB's second marriage, when he wed Florence Gilbert Dearholt and adopted her two kids Lee Chase and Caryl Lee. (Note that "Chase" forms a link with Wes's brother Eric Chase.) Or perhaps Texas Ann comes via ERB's son John Coleman Burroughs and his second wife Mary Nalon, which produced daughters Kimberly and Stacy, either one of which might be a public name for Texas Ann.

Such speculation was only speculation. Having surveyed the ERB side, it was time to press harder on the Texas Ann Burroughs side, specifically to find the names of her parents and see if they match the known grandchildren of ERB (Joanne Pierce, James Michael Pierce, John Ralston Burroughs, Danton Burroughs, Dian Burroughs, Kimberly Burroughs, Stacy Burroughs).

Luck is with us here, as *The Daily Register* (18 Sep 1958) tells of the wedding between Texas Ann Burroughs, daughter of Dr. and Mrs. E. W. Burroughs of Shawneetown, Illinois, to Melver Leonard Anderson Jr. of Houston, Texas. Also mentioned is Texas Ann's sister Rebecca, and her brother Edgar Wales.

This is an electrifying bit, since ERB was born and raised in the Chicago area. There is also the curious detail that Dr. Burroughs is probably named Edgar, just like ERB himself.

But there is more: *The Daily Register* (4 Nov 1958) tells of the passing of Dr. Burroughs's mother-in-law, Mrs. Texas Bates, who was 91 years of age. Furthermore, as Dr. Burroughs was married to Texas Burroughs, and named a daughter Texas Ann Burroughs, we have records of at least three generations of women named "Texas."

Finally, "Find a Grave" shows a headstone for Dr. Edgar W. Burroughs (1892–1976) that lists children Edgar W., Texas A., and Rebecca C. This seems to be the father of Texas Ann, and thus the grandfather of Wes Anderson. Note that Dr. Burroughs was born in 1892, which is eight years before ERB first married. Thus it seems impossible that ERB is father to Dr. Burroughs, and therefore ERB could not be great grandfather to Wes Anderson. True, ERB had older brothers George, Harry, and Frank, but none of them seem to have produced an Edgar Wales Burroughs, and even if one had, such a fellow would be a great granduncle to Wes Anderson.

The fact seems to be that Wes Anderson is the grandson of Edgar Wales Burroughs. "Edgar Wales Burroughs" sounds a bit like "Edgar Rice Burroughs," and maybe the notion of lineage between Wes and ERB started with such a simple slip.

An additional note on Dr. Burroughs and Wes Anderson is in order. Another biographical detail that Wes Anderson has given in many different interviews is that he was traumatized by the divorce of his parents in 1977, when he was in fourth grade. Anybody who has watched his movies will probably nod in understanding at this, since so much of his work has to do with fractured families. With this in mind, I note that Dr. Burroughs and his wife Texas both died in 1976: she in January, and he ten months later in October. To me this heightens the sense of crisis in the Anderson family in that era, and further emphasizes what a bad year 1976 was for them.

[Addendum: This piece was published in *New York Review of Science Fiction* (June, 2014). About a year later, the Edgar Rice Burroughs-focused publication *ERBzine* issue 5369 (September, 2015) told fans about a Familypedia page on ERB asserting that Wes Anderson is ERB's great-grand-nephew. That is, ERB's brother George was father of Edgar Wales Burroughs, who was father of Texas Ann Burroughs, who is mother of Wes Anderson.]

THREE MOVIES RESPONDING TO HITLER (1936 TO 1941)

As the decades roll by in the aftermath of World War Two, Hitler remains a potent figure of dread fascination in popular culture. Out of this rises the vexing question, "What did the United Kingdom and the United States think of Hitler before the war?" In part this is related to the perennial question, "Why didn't they stop Hitler earlier?"

One way to sample popular thought during the pre-war years is to examine motion pictures of the day. To that end, I elect three movies that responded to Hitler in different ways: the British feature *Things to Come* (1936), the American serial *Buck Rogers* (1939), and the American feature *Meet John Doe* (1941). The first two are science fiction, while the last is a political thriller/comedy drama. I showcase these three because they are all in the public domain, and they provide contrast with each other. They are not meant to be stand-ins for all pre-war movies responding to Hitler, but at the same time, none of them seem to have fallen outside of what was considered the normal sensibilities of their time.

To set the stage, it is important to review a few historical points within the period of these films.

Chronology

1933: Hitler is appointed chancellor of Germany.
1934: Hitler becomes head of state.
1936: Hitler reoccupies the Rhineland (western Germany).
1939: Hitler invades western Poland.
1940: World War Two begins.
1941: The USA enters the war in December.

The British motion picture *Things to Come* (1936) has a high pedigree, coming rather directly from H. G. Wells. It depicts a future history of 100 years in three distinct parts: the first has a general war beginning in 1940; the second shows a barbaric era in 1970; and the third reveals a technological utopia in 2035. Thus a cycle of crisis, decline, and birth.

Things to Come portrays Germany attacking the UK from the air on a very specific date: Christmas of 1940. The prescience of this guess for a starting date of the war is incredible: the movie opened in London on February 20, 1936; Hitler reoccupied the Rhineland in March of 1936; Hitler formed the Axis with Italy in October of 1936; and finally the Battle of Britain began in July of 1940, only five months earlier than depicted in the film. This shows that the British, or at least the British filmmakers, had a very clear view of Hitler's ambitions four years in advance.

The second part of *Things to Come* takes place in the post-apocalyptic world of 1970. Here in the tumbled ruins of Everytown, a strongman rules as a quasi-medieval lord. But all this changes one day when an airplane comes over from the continent and lands in a nearby field. Its pilot, a man wearing a futuristic black uniform, turns out to be a former citizen of Everytown who had gone away when the war broke out. The pilot meets the town engineer (the functional equivalent of a village blacksmith) and learns about the warlord (around 36 minutes in).

Pilot: So that's the sort of man your boss is. Not an unusual type. *Everywhere we find these little semi-military upstarts robbing and fighting. That's what endless warfare's led to —brigandage. What else could happen? But we who are all that are left of the old engineers and mechanics have pledged ourselves to salvage the world. We have the airways, all that's left of them. We have the seas. And we have ideas in common: the Brotherhood of Efficiency, the Freemasonry of Science. We're the last trustees of civilization when everything else has failed.*

Engineer: I've been waiting for this. <Rises.> I'm yours to command.

Pilot: Not mine, not mine. No more bosses. Civilization's to command.

While inspiring in all the usual science fictional terms, this episode is a bit off-putting for a number of reasons. The exotic, futuristic plane is a black flying wing that seems to draw inspiration from the Futurist art movement, an aesthetic connected with proto-fascism; the pilot's black uniform seems taken more directly from the wardrobes of Italian and German dictators (in contrast to a silvery suit, for example). Talk of rule by a cadre of technologically capable elites sounds technocratic at best, anti-democratic authoritarian in general, totalitarian at worst. Emphasis on top-down "efficiency" (in contrast to market driven efficiency, e.g. the evolution of the cell phone) also seems a bit chilling. All together, these details suggest that democracy is dead.

The British filmmakers get high marks for anticipating the war with Nazi Germany and nailing the starting year. On the other hand, it is disturbing that the hero of part two flies like a totalitarian, dresses like a totalitarian, and talks like a totalitarian. Thus, while recognizing Hitler's threat, the movie still presents Hitler as a semi-role model for the coming post-democratic age.

Hitler's ambitions became more clear when he took Czechoslovakia; "Buck Rogers" (1939) was a serial that same year. "Buck Rogers" was made for American boys. The movie serial was adapted from a comic serial that began in 1929, and one of the changes made is that the villain, originally a super-criminal called "Killer Kane," in film became "the Leader Kane," an obvious stand-in for Hitler.

After 20th century hero Buck Rogers and his friend Buddy are rescued from their crashed airship, they learn they have accidentally traveled through time (*Planet Outlaws*, starting about 6 minutes in):

> *Professor Huer: Rankin, we are witnesses to a scientific miracle. By means of a gas discovered by Professor Morgan, these two people [Buck and Buddy] have remained in a state of suspended animation for five hundred years.*
>
> *Buck: Five hundred years?!*

In short order they learn that a tyrant rules Earth's big cities, while the rebels, who discovered the time-sleepers, have only the Hidden City in the wilderness. Buck asks about this tyrant, so Dr. Huer shows them a spy television device with which they see Leader Kane in his council chambers, where a recently captured rebel is marched in to face questioning.

> *Kane: You may save yourself considerable discomfort by telling me where to find the entrance to the Hidden City.*
>
> *Agent: I do not remember.*
>
> *Kane: I think I know a way to make you remember.*

Kane uses a television device (note: television within television) to show the agent his future fate as a mind-numbed human robot. The agent still refuses to cooperate and is taken away.

Reacting to this, Buck asks Dr. Huer for further information.

> Buck: *I don't understand, sir. Who is this man called Killer Kane?*
>
> Professor Huer: *He is the result of the stupidity of the men of your century. You failed to stamp out lawlessness, and in the end, the criminal became stronger than the law. 'Racketeers' you called them. Today they rule the world as cruelly as they ruled their gangs in your day.*

While the film version changed the villain's name to "Leader Kane," still he is referred to as "Killer Kane," linking to the comic strip's criminal; and Professor Huer's guilt trip on the hapless time travelers is based upon lawlessness that their generation failed to halt in the 1930s. Though aimed at children, "Buck Rogers" is crystal clear with regard to Hitler as an enemy who must be stopped, not emulated. Yet the boys in the audience were too young to fight in the war when it broke out a couple of years later, so the warning was lost on them.

In 1940, FDR was elected to an unprecedented third term, pledging to keep the USA out of the war engulfing Europe. By that point Germany had taken western Poland, followed by conquest of Denmark, Sweden, Holland, and Belgium. Thus Hitler's war in Europe had already begun when *Meet John Doe* (1941) came out, but this cinematic reaction to Hitler is more concerned with the rise of an American Hitler, just as in *It Can't Happen Here* (1935) by Sinclair Lewis. Steinbeck's *The Grapes of Wrath* (1939) also deserves mention, since Steinbeck sketches a Californian fascist movement headed by the American Legion.

Meet John Doe is a Frank Capra film, and has many similarities to the better-known *It's a Wonderful Life* (1946). Still, rather than a Christmas movie it is a political thriller in which America, suffering the Great Depression, responds enthusiastically to a new populism from a man called "John Doe." John Doe Clubs spring up across the country, spreading like wildfire. John Doe meets with miners, farmers, and main street workers. As he travels across America he is met by enthusiastic parades. He is

Time magazine's "Man of the Year." The John Doe Club is stubbornly non-partisan: at around the one hour, eight minute mark we see first the Democratic Party and then the Republican Party express their inability to co-opt the movement.

A John Doe Convention is attended by fifteen thousand, with live radio coverage reaching across the nation. The crowd sings "The Battle Hymn of the Republic," a patriotic song, as they wait through the rain for their idol John Doe to arrive.

However, behind the scenes we see the first intimation of a conspiracy when the financial backer, a media mogul, reveals to a confidant that he intends John Doe to announce the formation of a third party, the John Doe Party, and then John Doe will nominate the mogul himself to be the party's first presidential candidate (1:18:00). Later, surrounded by his fat cat cronies, the mogul expands a bit upon his real politics: "These are daring times. We're coming to a new order of things. There's been too much talk going on in this country. Too many concessions have been made. What the American people need is an iron hand" (1:33:00).

John Doe arrives at the packed stadium (at around 1:39:00). Signs held aloft show names of states, indicating that delegates are present. Enthusiasm is high, despite the rain pouring down. The crowd sings the happy, nonsensical folksong "Oh! Susanna," their rising umbrellas and their stomping feet keeping time. But now, with the betrayal coming, all the happiness bleeds out for the hero John Doe and the viewers of the movie. The nonsense of "Oh! Susanna" seems nightmarish in the ruins of the grassroots dream, and in hindsight, the earlier "Battle Hymn of the Republic" was a tune of the Civil War, hinting now at new bloodshed about to come. We are left with a stark stand-in for a torchlight Nazi rally, where the bouncing of the umbrellas mirror straight-arm "Sieg Heil" salutes, where "patriotism" is merely a mask for sinister forces of brutality.

In this way the movie presents Hitler as being dangerous due to his potential as a model for domestic imitators, rather than due to his actual ongoing conquest of Europe.

If *Things to Come* had remarkably good timing with unfolding historical events, *Meet John Doe* had very bad timing.

Meet John Doe was released in May, 1941.

Seven months later, America entered the war against Hitler.

During the war, Capra made a dozen documentaries about the conflict, memorable for their "Why we fight" bit, beginning with *Prelude to War* (1942), and ending with *Here is Germany* (1945).

Granted, recent scholarship has discovered the political censorship leveraged by Nazi Germany upon Hollywood, in Doherty's *Hollywood and Hitler, 1933–1939* (2013). So it might well be the case that these three movies are showing the limits of what might be expressed under such Nazi oversight. From other sources it appears that a 1936 movie version of Sinclair Lewis's *It Can't Happen Here* was suppressed by Nazi pressure, which perhaps makes it more subversive that *Meet John Doe* could come so close to the same theme and yet still be made.

Hollywood and Hitler claims that the secret Nazi-Soviet pact in August 1939 broke Hollywood's reluctance to be critical of Hitler. Hollywood began putting out anti-Nazi movies in the remaining 15 months of pre-war time, films like Chaplin's *The Great Dictator* (1940), Hitchcock's *Foreign Correspondent* (1940), and Borzage's *The Mortal Storm* (1940). The change was so pronounced that in September 1941 the U.S. Senate held hearings on Hollywood's explicitly anti-Nazi and pro-interventionist stance.

These points do not much affect my argument, except that *Meet John Doe* seems even more odd, sticking out like a sore thumb when Hollywood's tide had turned against Hitler. So it would seem that the clarity offered by historical hindsight greatly obscures how muddled things really are in the current moment of the times, such that Hitler is seen in one case as a semi-role model for the coming era of post-democracy; in another case as a super-villain fit for children; and in a third case as a bad role model for impressionable malcontents being manipulated by economic royalists.

SF ROCK: THE HUMAN LEAGUE

The Human League is a band that began in the late 1970s with science fiction storytelling, but only gained popularity after transitioning to catchy dance music. This is a tale of a move from the gritty ghetto to the delightful disco, or from "pavement" to "penthouse."

The Human League formed in 1977 Sheffield as a new wave band. That their name comes from an SF wargame, "Starforce: Alpha Centauri," proves a geek reference point. The four young men were heavily into electronic music of an avant-garde nature, yet they generally avoided the cold robotic sound of Germany's Kraftwerk, moving more toward the witty whimsy of Brian Eno, with stormy emotions from the punk rock scene.

One result was a sort of SF storytelling, as if music hall numbers like "Mack the Knife" were made from genre tales, or if SF radio drama were set to futuristic music. Thus, the League's first album *Reproduction* (1979) gives us:

- "Almost Medieval," a Ballardian stroll through shifting timeframes and surrealist sensibilities where contact lenses grow up into spectacles. Notable for being dark and brooding, the singer is describing how his lover's soul triggers a time-regression in him.

- "Circus of Death," an episode of "Hawaii Five-O" that morphs into existential dread before ending with a two-line clip from the SF black comedy film "Dark Star" (1974). By turns playful, dark, pleading, and grimly humorous.

• "Empire State Human," wherein the narrator embarks upon a self-improvement regimen of growing himself brick by brick into the biggest person.

So a third of the nine songs are SF stories. The other tracks include a driving teen anthem with catchy hooks ("Blind Youth") and a cover song ("You've Lost that Lovin' Feelin'").
The album was a commercial failure.

The League tried again, with *Travelogue* (1980), which gives us:

• "The Black Hit of Space," where the witness tells of a tune from the stars that leads to the destruction of the world before he can finish his sandwich. Note the irreverent, mocking attitude: describing the song's rise through the charts, he says, "It got to number one, then into minus figures. Though nobody could understand why."

• "Dreams of Leaving," a party member of an Orwellian state wants to get out.

• "Crow and a Baby," a nursery room nightmare turns into a cipher for a relationship between the singer and his girlfriend.

• "W.X.J.L. Tonight," with a disc jockey, the last on Earth, who tells of the radio broadcast culture in the past, before robots took over. Sort of a *Fahrenheit 451* for rock music, in a way.

Forty percent of the tracks are storytelling. The other six songs include a cover ("Only After Dark") that shows new melodic abilities approaching pop, and two instrumentals. There is also "The

Touchables," which has a frothy, catchy chorus.

These seven storytelling songs explore a strange area, but a few things become clear: "the kids can't dance to it," and at best they are novelty songs.

The Human League's third album, *Dare* (1981), marks a break in personnel and in sound: half of the band (the SF geeks) left to form a new group, "Heaven Seventeen" (name taken from fictional pop band in *A Clockwork Orange*, a relative geek downshift); two female singers came onboard; and the League style shifted to dance music. But despite these huge changes, its big breakout hit, "Don't You Want Me," seems to be a composite created from strong elements the band had created before, being a story song with a dark and brooding mode (male singer), a light, irreverent mode (female singer), and a frothy, catchy chorus (both singers). This time the story is not drawing influence from SF but from the tragic love story of *A Star is Born*.

In contrast to such popstars as David Bowie and Gary Numan, who launched their careers using SF tropes, The Human League was not able to achieve liftoff until they had abandoned their SF baggage.

BALLARD'S DEBT TO HAWTHORNE

"Prima Belladonna"

The Ascent of Wonder (1994) by Hartwell and Cramer taught me many things, but the most startling was that the familiar Ballard story "Prima Belladonna" (1956) was based on a Hawthorne story I had never read: "Rappaccini's Daughter" (1844). I do not know who first traced this connection, but I am enthused enough, even after all these years, to compare and contrast the two works.

Basically the pattern is Boy meets Girl; Girl is Monster; Death comes; Boy is Sad.

Set in Italy sometime centuries in the past, "Rappaccini's Daughter" casts the Boy as Giovanni, a young college student whose rental apartment overlooks a secluded garden. This botanical oasis is really the laboratory of mad scientist Rappaccini, and his beautiful daughter Beatrice is the Girl. The mad doctor collects and creates noxious plants, one of which is so virulent that it can kill with a drop of sap or even with airborne scent. It turns out that beautiful Bea is his greatest creation, a sister to that most deadly purple plant, and she can kill with a simple touch or a breath. But she is a nice girl; a good girl.

Giovanni has a protector in this town, a family friend named Baglioni, a good doctor who is locked in rivalry with the Faustian Rappaccini. Baglioni warns Giovanni about Beatrice, but then when there is no talking the lover out of his love, he gives the boy a phial containing a powerful antidote to poison. The good doctor says this will cure the girl.

Giovanni is skeptical, but then a new crisis emerges as he discovers his touch withers plants, and his breath kills a spider: he has been transformed by proximity to the deadly "bella donna." He confronts Beatrice, who weeps. The mad scientist appears and pronounces them a new race of man. Beatrice, rejecting her father's dream, drinks the potion and dies, alas! Baglioni appears for a triumphant yell at the old man: "and is *this* the upshot of your experiment?" (85)

Ballard's "Prima Belladonna" is set in the near future in a weird desert resort land called Vermillion Sands. It was the first of his professionally published stories, and the first of nine stories set in this location. The Boy here is the narrator Steve, a playboy who lives above his music shop where he sells singing plants. One day on his balcony, he and his two beer buddies get an eyeful of a new Girl in town, the gorgeous Jane Ciracylides. (Thus a few reversals: the garden is his; she is the stranger in town.)

Jane, they quickly admit, is a bit of a "mutant," with her golden skin and her "insects for eyes." All the men find her very alluring. She is a singer on tour.

Steve's shop has a temperamental orchid, a "diva" if you will, that he uses to train and exercise the other plants. When Jane visits the first time, the orchid reacts very badly, nearly ruining the whole shop's $10,000 worth of stock until Steve tranquilizes it.

Jane's opening night at the Casino wows the town, but Steve's orchid is still agitated and he loses $300 in shrubs the next day. Over the next four days he fights a losing battle. Jane offers to help out on a special order by using her voice to train and exercise the plants, i.e., replace the temperamental diva. She proves to be so successful he admits she is better than the orchid and offers her a job. She wants to try singing with the orchid. He says maybe tomorrow, and they have sex.

Then follows a honeymoon period as a couple, until the last night when he catches her singing in mortal combat with the orchid. Figuring it out at last, he leaves them to it, even keeping his buddies from "rescuing" her.

When the music stops, the three go in to find her, but she is gone. The next day the orchid dies. Jane is rumored to have been seen in the next town.

Steve ends this gothic opera on a wry note: "So if any of you around here keep a choro-florist's, and have a Khan-Arachnid orchid, look out for a golden-skinned woman with insects for eyes. Perhaps she'll play i-Go with you, and I'm sorry to have to say it, but she'll always cheat" (332).

Comparing The Two Stories

Hartwell writes that Hawthorne's story "is one of the founding documents in the depiction of the doctor and the scientist as devoted to (and sometimes perverted by) science and the quest for knowledge" (68). In this case, "a handsome young man . . . becomes a pawn in the rivalry between two ambitious scientists" (68).

We speak of "the birds and the bees" with regard to reproductive strategies in order to get around the more mammalian passions by focusing on the passionless plants, who reproduce through the labor of birds and bees.

"Rappaccini's Daughter" uses "birds and bees," actually a lizard and an insect, to prove how lethal this garden is through their deaths. The corollary is that Beatrice is the only one who can tend to them: she is "the birds and the bees" in a single, unique form.

As Hartwell states, this is a Faustian story, meaning the garden is not evil because Nature can be evil, it is made evil through evil science. So while the lovers find themselves in a "Romeo and Juliet" scenario, they are pawns in a rivalry. This makes thematic sense, good science versus evil science, but I feel the triumphalism of the last line is awkward and problematic: Baglioni is accessory to murder, and he dares to shout a put-down to the victim's father? Such bravado raises the suspicion that Baglioni knew the antidote would kill the girl, making him worse than Rappaccini.

Hartwell writes "'Prima Belladonna' is Hawthorne's 'Rappaccini's Daughter' transformed, an injection of Gothic sensibility and perverse sexuality into a literature (and to an audience) unprepared" (323).

Indeed. Ballard uses the same "first view of Girl is from a balcony," and then heightens the voyeurism by strongly implying that Jane is nude except for a hat. Likewise, even though Ballard switches song for scent, still he writes, "I felt curiously sleepy, almost sick on the air she's left behind" (331).

But there is no Faust in Ballard's story, it is pure Nature. Jane is both "bird" (she sings) and "bee" (her insects for eyes), but these are cute masks for a monster that is more accurately a singing spider woman. She is not a sister to a plant, as Beatrice is, she is a female insect along the lines of a black widow or a preying mantis. Ballard had set this up by including, among a drawer's-worth of outrageous scientific detail, this rather more somber and sober bit: "The orchid took its name from the . . . spider which pollinated the flower, simultaneously laying its own eggs in the fleshy ovule" (326).

Thus, Jane is a spider, and what looks like "fighting" is an act of DNA exchange rather more savage than the mammalian rite. So the mating ritual of song and dance ends in a violent act. This time it is the plant that dies, and presumably the girl carries its pollen away to use herself or upon another plant. (One wonders if the dead orchid bears the living embryonic offspring of Jane and Steve.)

But there is even more: a Ballardian pun that goes something like, "She sexed me but took away my testicles," where "orchid" is Greek for testicles. Again validating Jane's female insect aspect, but also putting "birds and bees" into a blender with "the war of the sexes."

RAVING ON "THE REPAIRER OF REPUTATIONS"

This is an examination of the first story in *The King in Yellow* (1895), a book by Robert W. Chambers that inspired Lovecraft's Cthulhu Mythos in the 20th century and shows up in the TV cop drama "True Detectives" in the 21st century. After a brief synopsis of the tale, I will plunge into what I intuit to be the physical inspiration for the story, and then I will unmask the hidden author of the fabled play "The King in Yellow."

"The Repairer of Reputations" is set in a New York City of what was then the future date of 1921. It is written by Hildred Castaigne, who starts his narrative with the day he was released from a four-year stay at the insane asylum after a fall from his horse. The day of his release happened to be the day the first Government Lethal Chamber (a free suicide booth) was opened with fanfare on Washington Square Park.

Hildred, who has an apartment facing the park, visits his friend Mr. Wilde, a bizarre eccentric who lives a few blocks away. Wilde has recently begun a new career as a "repairer of reputations," but his main project with Hildred is the establishment of an American imperial dynasty, having Hildred as the first emperor, who will rule on Earth as vassal to, and representative of, the mysterious otherworldly King in Yellow. (This lord is the subject of a notorious play, "The King in Yellow," which is widely rumored to cause insanity among those who read it.)

The chief problem of Hildred and Mr. Wilde is that, according to their extensive genealogical studies, Hildred's cousin Louis is the rightful heir to the throne. So Hildred's task is to convince Louis to renounce the crown and swear to never marry, upon threat of death.

Naturally, Louis knows nothing of this, and gets himself a fiancée.

At this crisis point, Mr. Wilde calls forth an unwilling client named Vance to act as assassin, and Hildred signs the death warrant against the young woman and her father, who live downstairs in the same building as Mr. Wilde. Hildred then goes forth to convince his cousin Louis, who, upon hearing him out, reasonably thinks the whole thing is insane. After Hildred sees the assassin Vance dash into the nearby suicide chamber, he suggests to his cousin that the girl is now dead, and Louis chases him to the building. Hildred goes upstairs to don his regal attire and consult with Wilde, only to find that Wilde has been murdered. He suspects the house cat; the police, who burst in and arrest Hildred after a madman struggle, clearly suspect him; as do Louis, his fiancée, and her father, also on the scene. The story ends with an editor's note that the author Hildred "died yesterday in the Asylum for the Criminally Insane."

So the story, after playing with the tension between "tale of conspiracy" and "tale of insanity," concludes on the side of "insanity," and yet does so in such a way as to make the conspiracy reading more likely. Or better yet, why chose between the two, when it can be a tale of genuine conspiracy and cosmic insanity?

"The Repairer of Reputations" is a marvel, a tour de force. It draws heavy elements from Edgar Allan Poe, lighter bits from Ambrose Bierce. It defies genre: A mystery story that is not solved correctly (it seems likely that Vance killed Wilde). A thriller about a masterful conspiracy to take over the USA that is thwarted, not by the efforts of a dogged hero, but by treachery from a loose cannon (if Vance killed Wilde). A future history in which all the meticulous details, eerily prescient, are just garnish. It is a story in a book, yet it ends with an editorial note as if it were published in a current periodical (a tactic which still deftly refuses to give a true date year for the frame tale). It has a narrator who reveals elements of delusional insanity, but his friend Mr. Wilde, who speaks of even greater insanity, has enough surprising details verified as "true" by outsiders, that we are left with the uneasy belief that he always tells the truth: thus the logic puzzles involving a traveler meeting the Indian who lies some of the time and the Indian who tells only the truth.

The remaining nine stories in the book give very few clues about the situation in "The Repairer of Reputations." Only one, "The Yellow Sign," is set in New York City; mostly they are placed in Paris or the French countryside. None of them are explicitly set in the 1920s, so the default date is 1895, with one case ("The Street of the First Shell") set in the 1870 Siege of Paris.

Here, then, are the clues. The story "The Mask" tells of the sculptor Boris Yvain, whose work "the Fates" adorns the government suicide chamber, thus verifying that there is a work of that name by that artist. The story "The Yellow Sign" makes reference to "the awful tragedy of young Castaigne," but when the narrator walks through Washington Square Park he passes the statue of Garibaldi, an artwork which in the "Repairer" timeline was replaced in 1897; and the narrator talks to a young man who had fought at the battle of Tel el-Kebir (1882).

The timeline paradox of "Repairer" comes down to the question of what year it really is in the frame tale: Either it is in the 1920s, or it is in the 1890s and all that "future" stuff, including the suicide booth, is only a symptom of Hildred's insanity. On the side of 1920s, it seems like outsiders verify elements and point out inconsistencies with Hildred's imperial regalia. Then again, while we do not know Hildred's year of birth, he and his cousin seem to be about the same age, perhaps in their mid-twenties; yet we are told his cousin's birth year is 1877, and 1921 minus 1877 equals 44 years old. While this might not be too old for a military bachelor to be seeking a young bride, it plays havoc with "the awful tragedy of *young* Castaigne." Still, at the same time 1895 minus 1877 equals 18 years old, which might be good enough for cousin Louis, yet if Hildred is the same age, then he began his four years of mental monitoring at 14, which seems far too young. Granted, Hildred might be a few years older than Louis, and such an age gap between young men (say, four years) might explain some of their banter with each other.

Perhaps Chambers set out to create obfuscation, but I tend to doubt that. In my reading, the paradox resolves in another "both" answer: Hildred is living in both 1895 and 1921 at the same time. Maybe this future timeline will come physically true once he has taken the throne, but for him, somehow, it is already true enough for interaction.

Part of the reason I come up with this is, again, looking at other stories in the book. There is one where the guy is walking in the French countryside and he meets a woman speaking an antique form of French... you know how that one goes. So anyway, what I am proposing for Hildred is the opposite of that trope, a guy who bridges present and future in a mazy sort of way.

Intuiting The Physical Inspiration

Robert W. Chambers grew up in Brooklyn, and as a young man he studied art in Paris from 1886 to 1893. After some early success in visual arts (sales to magazines *Life*, *Truth*, and *Vogue*), he abruptly turned to writing in 1887. His first book was a novel; his second was *The King in Yellow*.

So it should come as no surprise that "Repairer" is full of artistic details, from statues to gardens to sunlight on cathedrals, etc. The details he gives on Washington Square are so fine that I can map the locations and character movements with incredible accuracy. He lightly touches upon the "Washington Memorial Arch" [sic] three times, and I believe that this monumental structure is what inspired him to write the story.

That is to say, Chambers had lived in Paris; he knew firsthand the Arc de Triomphe, a monument marking the transition from republic to empire. I am proposing that the sight of the Washington Arch (completed in 1892, while he was away) struck him with all that Napoleonic baggage. At one point in the story, cousin Louis visits Hildred's apartment: "He glanced along the row of shelves. 'Napoleon, Napoleon, Napoleon!' he read. 'For heaven's sake, have you nothing but Napoleon there?'"

Chambers was a fan of Poe, and just as the standard American phrase "Indian Summer" launched Poe to write his story "A Tale of the Ragged Mountains," so I suppose that the imperialistic invasion of Manhattan's artists' quarter triggered for Chambers the logical shadow of a Napoleonic/Prussian styled empire in America.

The Playwright Of The King In Yellow

Throughout the book the author of the notorious drama is alluded to, but never named. In "Repairer," cousin Louis says, "I believe the author shot himself after bringing forth this monstrosity, didn't he?" To which Hildred replies, "I understand he is still alive."

This is interesting for two reasons. First, there is a case in another story, "The Mask," where a named artist shoots himself after working on a named piece of art. This detail adds to the echo-chamber nature of the book as a whole. The other thing is that Hildred hints he knows more.

Hildred is not the only fan of the play in the story: there is also Mr. Wilde, the eccentric, and Mr. Vance, the assassin. But that is not quite right, since Vance is not exactly a "fan," as evidenced when he cries out to Hildred, "I am broken down—I was in a madhouse and now—when all was coming right—when I had forgotten the King—the King in Yellow and—but I shall go mad again—I shall go mad—" So Vance is more properly a thrall.

The play is one of two texts used by the conspirators: the other text is a manuscript titled "The Imperial Dynasty of America," which traces the bloodline from Carcosa, the land of the King in Yellow, to America, where it is represented by Louis and Hildred. So while the play is about the strange doom that befell Carcosa, the genealogy points toward a successful transplant in

North America.

The name of the story "The Repairer of Reputations" refers to Mr. Wilde, making him the titular hero. Wilde has only recently taken on this profession: what he had done previously remains unknown. Constance, beloved of cousin Louis, says of Wilde, "it must be hard to live alone year after year poor, crippled and almost demented"; whereas her father says, "I think he is vicious."

Mr. Wilde's face is yellow. He has no ears, and to compensate for this he wears artificial ones made of pink wax, held in place by fine wires. His left hand has no fingers. He is "very small, scarcely higher than a child of ten," but his arms are "magnificently developed, and his thighs as thick as any athelete's."

Hildred goes on to write, "Still, the most remarkable thing about Mr. Wilde was that a man of his marvelous intelligence and knowledge should have such a head. It was flat and pointed, like the head of those unfortunates whom people imprison in asylums for the weak-minded."

This character is so vividly bizarre that he seems a gothic figure, a mad monk or a sinister villain. The shape of his head marks him as a circus freak; but the lack of ears and half his fingers seem more like the result of mutilations meted out by a more medieval culture for some sort of terrible crime deserving less than the death penalty. If his ears were cropped, this was to mark him as a dangerous criminal; if his fingers were removed, perhaps he had committed counterfeiting or forgery with them.

I strongly suspect that Mr. Wilde is the author of the play. I believe his authorship is the crime for which he was punished with mutilation. The fact that his face is "yellow" is not insignificant; nor that he has lost the digits of his left hand, the "sinister" one.

Cousin Louis says of the play, "I don't care if the thing is, as they say, the very supreme essence of art. It's a crime to have written it."

"Repairer" And The Rest Of The Book

Many readers have noted that "Repairer" starts the book off with a bang, a thunderclap that echoes in the next story, then echoes more softly, then whispers, and then is no more. That is, the book begins in weird gothic genre, then by stages dilutes that with romance genre until there is nothing but "boy meets girl" romance at the end.

It is a disappointing reading experience, rather like a "bait and switch" con game, but I think it is true to the subsequent career of Chambers as a best-selling writer of romances.

Because Chambers had such training as an artist, and because the structure of the book seems so thematically strong, I suspect that *The King in Yellow* is something like a "book of love" patterned on Ovid's *Metamorphoses*, an arrangement of case studies. "Repairer" has no love interest for the narrator: in fact, he is a sort of black cupid trying to separate the lovers. While love is a kind of madness, insanity is the absence of love. But all the other stories pivot on love interests, and by the last story, mundane love is magical and precious.

His first book, *In the Quarter* (1894), is a lot like the TV show "Friends" set in the Paris of the 1890s rather than the New York City of the 1990s. It is a messed-up mess. There are fannish allusions to Poe, but only as garnish, no substance. There is an international conspiracy of blackmailers that matches the repairer of reputations, but they are stereotypical villains who are only in it for the money and the evil fun.

So I think that Chambers set out to purge himself after this first book. He purged himself of flabby dithering and produced sharp short stories. He purged himself of Poe by writing the substance of weird gothic, thereby bumping up against the inherent limitations: A tale revealed in the end to be that of a madman; another revealed to be that of a man on his deathbed; another that is a dream within a dream; a time-travel romance; a powerful prose poem; and so on.

From the power lust insanity of a solitary man, to the tender heart of a man in love.

NOTES ON "THE PROPHETS' PARADISE"

of The King in Yellow

Robert Chambers's book *The King in Yellow* (1895) is a work made up of ten sections, all of them being short stories except for one, so-called "The Prophets' Paradise," which is a collection of one poem and eight prose-poem vignettes. Located near the center of the book, this section strikes me as being choppy, in high contrast to the languid nature of the stories. As a 1902 review in *The New York Times* stated, "it must be confessed that 'The Prophets' Paradise,' being weird, mystical, and disjointed, is somewhat difficult of interpretation." Indeed; the vignettes use forceful poetic images, a hypnotic use of repetition, and surprising twists. Rather like a kaleidoscope of sense and sensations.

It is a weird experimental art interlude in the book. The reason for its inclusion is mysterious.

The section comes as sixth of the ten, located between the weird story "The Demoiselle d'Ys" and the creepy mundane tale "The Street of the Four Winds," maybe marking the break in the book between the weird and the mundane. I do not think that "The Prophets' Paradise" is really the group name, I think that is only the name of the opening poem. With this adjustment, there are nine poems, which gives a strong hint that each poem relates to one of the stories.

Aside from the possible poem-to-story angle, the piece has a compelling cohesion as a whole if one looks beyond the initial impression of nightmarish stasis. That is, the opening poem gives a philosophical overture; "The Studio" describes an artist in self-imposed exile, waiting on Love to arrive; "The Phantom" has two people halted on a path; "The Sacrifice" gives a repetition of growing horror without escape; and so on. But one can see the whole as a sort of "pilgrim's progress" for one struggling artist.

The section opens with "The Prophets' Paradise," a poem in the style of *Rubaiyat of Omar Khayyam:*

> "If but the Vine and Love Abjuring Band
> Are in the Prophets' Paradise to stand,
> Alack, I doubt the Prophets' Paradise,
> Were empty as the hollow of one's hand."

The meaning seems to be:

> If only those who renounce Wine and Love
> Are allowed within the Prophets' Paradise
> Regretful, I doubt the place itself
> And guess it to be as empty as an open hand.

Here is a sketch of how the thing goes:

1. "The Prophets' Paradise": this is about Love (and "Wine"?)

2. "The Studio": the Artist hears the call to seek Love beyond his studio but he chooses to wait for Love.

3. "The Phantom": the Artist travels with the Phantom of the Past and forgets, just as she says he will. Forgetting, he leaves her behind.

4. "The Sacrifice": the Artist sees the weeping Murderess with her jar of blood from her lover.

5. "Destiny": the Artist arrives at the bridge that few may pass,

and is told to cross. He laughs and lingers to watch many try. Then the crowd says he is too late, but he laughs and enters the bridge.

6. "The Throng": the Artist and Pierrot banter in a crowd, then Truth tries to help.

7. "The Jester": the Clown talks about how the Murderess stabbed the lover who had searched for her for so long.

8. "The Green Room": the Artist, the Clown, and Death sit before a mirror.

9. "The Love Test": the Artist, Love, and the Beloved.

Even if the poems do not map to stories, the whole still shares the pattern of returning back to the beginning, just as the stories do: in "The Love Test" the Beloved says "Teach me to wait," which cycles back to the waiting on Love in "The Studio"; in just such a way as the story "Rue Barrée" cycles back to the madness of the first story, "The Repairer of Reputations," but now it is the madness of Love.

Still, I am curious as to how the poems match the stories.

1. "The Prophets' Paradise": "The Repairer of Reputations" (world without Love)

2. "The Studio": "The Mask" (studio with alchemical fluid)

3. "The Phantom": "In the Court of the Dragon" (artist chased by a ghost)

4. "The Sacrifice": "The Yellow Sign" (couple doomed by an artifact)

5. "Destiny": "The Demoiselle d'Ys" (time-crossed lovers)

6. "The Throng": "The Street of the Four Winds" (necrophilia)

7. "The Jester": "The Street of the First Shell" (young couple in wartime)

8. "The Green Room": "The Street of Our Lady of the Fields" (budding romance)

9. "The Test": "Rue Barrée" (Love must wait)

Some of the links are strong. "The Prophets' Paradise" and "The Repairer of Reputations" (note the pattern of alliteration) align in the grim, lonely world without Love. "The Mask" has a strong location in the alchemical studio; and more importantly, the true love returns to life in that studio, fulfilling the promise in "The Studio." "Destiny" seems a theme of "The Demoiselle d'Ys"; and the ending of "Love must wait" seems fitting for the final two.

Other links are weaker. "In the Court of the Dragon" has a phantom, but it seems quite different from the winsome spirit of "The Phantom"; "The Yellow Sign" uses the word "sacrifice," but the action is more an accident; and the gory war scenes of "The Street of the First Shell" find some similarity to the Clown talking about stabbing in "The Jester" (making the Murderess into France mourning her beloved soldiers). "The Street of Four Winds" has a sort of "throng" in that the hero meets several men (a janitor, a butcher, a baker, a sculptor) who seem to know the mysterious woman he seeks; and the green room finds an echo in the green forest the couple heads toward with exhilaration at the end.

This altercation between strong and weak links might also form a pattern.

1. Strong
2. Strong
3. Weak
4. Weak
5. Strong
6. Weak
7. Weak
8. Weak
9. Strong

Chambers is playing a game here. While the first half of his book *The King in Yellow* has the nebulous play called "The King in Yellow" lurking in the background, glimpsed in scattered fragments, at the center of the book he has this section "The Prophets' Paradise" (another title doubling) that appears to be a blueprint for the whole book in concentrated, baffling miniatures.

SPIKE & SOFIA: THEIR WAR

(in Three Movies)

To the American public, Hollywood celebrities and their outsized lives are like classical gods. These media figures seem to take their personal-made-public drama all too lightly, suggesting that the sordid details are just water off a duck's back, but perhaps in rare occasion we might glimpse something real in their work. I have a theory about the war between Spike Jonze and Sofia Coppola that is chronicled through three movies: *Being John Malkovich* (1999), *Lost in Translation* (2003), and *Her* (2013).

Let's begin with the biographical facts that Spike and Sofia were married in 1999 and divorced, without children, in 2003. Sofia subsequently had a baby (2006), then another (2010), before marrying their father in 2011.

The year 1999 was a big one for Spike and Sofia since, in addition to their wedding, it saw the release of two first films: hers (*The Virgin Suicides*) and his (*Being John Malkovich*). Both directors were young and talented. Sofia is third generation film family; Spike is a scrappy outsider who gained fame through directing music videos. At first their marriage seemed to be a meeting of equals, but then, apparently, it went bad.

Spike's *Being John Malkovich* is a science fiction film that blends "Twilight Zone" with art house. It begins with a married couple Craig and Lotte, where he is a street puppeteer and she is a pet store clerk. Both bring their work home, which means their apartment is part puppet workshop and part zoo. Marital tension is signaled in a scene where Lotte says she wants to have children, but Craig answers he is not ready yet. Then Craig meets the Other Woman, Maxine, and falls in lust with her; soon after, Lotte meets Maxine and also falls in lust with her. This love triangle is further complicated by some non-consensual body-switching with the Other Man, during which Craig crosses a line or three into Evil. In the end, though, Craig is condemned to silently watch the two women together raise their child, happily ever after. He is a cuckold prisoner, rather like a Titan trapped within a personalized Hell.

Sofia's *Lost in Translation* is a non-genre film, a drama/romance about Platonic Love. Here the married couple is John, a fashion photographer, and Charlotte, a philosophy graduate. They are in an exotic foreign city (Tokyo) for his job, where Charlotte feels neglected by John and gets hints he has been unfaithful with the Other Woman they bump into. Charlotte meets and befriends the Other Man, Bob, an older, fading American actor who is there for his own photo shoot. The young wife and the old husband have a relationship that they struggle to keep Platonic, resulting in something like a Father/Daughter friendship. Early on, Bob resists the seductions of a pre-paid Japanese prostitute, but then this Other Man has a tryst with a different Other Woman. This seems a double betrayal, of both Bob's wife back in Los Angeles and Charlotte. After Charlotte argues with Bob over this, she leaves him for good, and the ending tone is so downbeat it seems plausible she will divorce John as well. While *Lost in Translation* is rather close to Kar-Wai Wong's masterful Hong Kong period piece *In the Mood for Love* (2000), Sofia's ambiguous ending avoids the tragic conclusion to *In the Mood for Love*.

Here is a mid-point recap of the war between Spike and Sofia: Spike's *Being John Malkovich* starts it by depicting a troubled marriage that descends to dissolution. To be clear, this movie was not written by Spike, and by itself it does not seem particularly related to Spike's life. In contrast, Sofia both wrote and directed *Lost in Translation,* and it seems deeply personal: the husband and wife are meant to be seen as Spike and Sofia. Furthermore, Sofia's film has links to *Being John Malkovich:* there is strong similarity between the names of the wife characters "Charlotte" (of *Lost in Translation*) and "Lotte" (of *Being John Malkovich*); the "unfaithful" aroma around John/Spike in *Lost in Translation* seems connected in the film to the actress of John's previous project, a pointer to Cameron Diaz (who played "Lotte" in Spike's *Being John Malkovich*). With an eye on the timeline of their marriage, *Lost in Translation* seems to be Sofia's "divorce movie."

The final film of this hypothetical (or "subliminal") trilogy is Spike's *Her* (2013), a near-future genre film that might be considered slipstream. This time the husband Theodore is a writer and the wife Catherine has a PhD in some sort of hard science (at one point Theodore refers to "that paper you wrote on synaptic behavioral routines"). They have been separated for nearly a year and she wants a divorce, but he is not ready to sign the papers. Then Theodore falls in love with the Other Woman, an emergent A.I. named Samantha, but he is not unique in this condition since human/A.I. love is becoming a social phenomenon. Theodore finally signs the divorce papers. Samantha brings in a different Other Woman to act as her physical surrogate for coitus (an upgrade from their usual telephonic form), but the experiment ends in disaster. Then Samantha reveals the Platonic relationship she is having with the Other Man, an older A.I. based upon Alan Watts (a real philosopher who died in 1973). Theodore feels neglected, but then Samantha and all the other A.I.s go away from Earth, leaving him abandoned.

Her is a tragedy form of Pygmalion: in that myth, Love wins as a sculptor's beloved statue is granted life, whereas in *Her* the hero commits all and loses all. Just as *Lost in Translation* ends without settling the basic question, the ending of *Her* might be seen as optimistic (hero climbing up out of an emotional hole) or pessimistic (hero jumps off building). The pessimistic hints are that his closure letter to ex-wife Catherine seems a bit suicidal; the shots of Theodore on the top of the building have an ominous edge of danger to them; and the ambient city sounds while the credits roll include the siren of an emergency vehicle.

In the same way that *Lost in Translation* seems a direct response to *Being John Malkovich*, so does *Her* seem to draw elements from *Lost in Translation*. The character of the wife seems similar: "Charlotte the philosophy grad" and "Catherine the Ph.D. (of something cerebral)." The voice actress for the A.I. Samantha is Scarlett Johansson, the same actress who previously played "Charlotte" in *Lost in Translation*. The futuristic city of *Her* seems like a blend of Los Angeles and a Chinese metropolis, producing something like the Shanghai glimpsed in the genre film *Looper* (2012), but I think it really owes more to the Tokyo of *Lost in Translation*. The pre-paid prostitute scene in *Lost in Translation* is replicated with the attempted surrogate scene in *Her*. The Other Man in both films is older (Bob the actor and Alan the A.I.). Spike even seems to drill down into Sofia's source of inspiration, going so far as to provide for *Her* an ending that is closer to Wong's *In the Mood for Love*, one-upping Sofia on that count.

The failure of Platonic Love is the same in all three films. It turns out that *Being John Malkovich* has an important early scene regarding Platonic Love: the husband Craig performs a puppet show about the famous medieval lovers Abelard and Heloise, who are known to us mainly through the powerful letters they wrote to each other. But rather than being the epitome of Tragic Love, Craig's version casts it as a Platonic Love wherein the monk and nun, from separate cells, write spicy letters to each other:

> *Heloise: While we enjoyed the pleasures of an uneasy love and abandoned ourselves to fornication, we were spared God's severity.*
>
> *Abelard: Say no more, I beg you, and cease from complaints like these which are so far removed from the true depths of love.*
>
> *Heloise: Even during the celebration of Mass, when our prayers should be pure, lewd visions of these pleasures take*

> such a hold upon my unhappy soul that my thoughts are on their very wantonness, instead of my prayers. Sometimes my thoughts are betrayed by the movement of my body.
>
> Abelard: I took my fill of my wretched pleasures in you, and this was the sum total of my love.

Following this, Craig has the puppets act out lewd movements, thus reducing the whole thing to medieval "phone sex." (In the movie a young girl on a street corner witnesses the performance, and her irate father beats Craig.)

To explain what a grotesque parody this is requires a few facts about Abelard and Heloise. Heloise was a famous scholar in Paris, where her family had standing; Abelard was a rapidly rising scholar from rustic Brittany. They began an affair in the year AD 1115. As a result, she gave birth; at which point Abelard talked her into a secret marriage. Unfortunately, her relatives were not happy with his treatment of Heloise, and they had him castrated. Abelard convinced Heloise to become a nun, after which he became a monk. They had no contact until around AD 1130, when their letters began. This, then, is the context for their letters: from the distance of many years they are looking back with mixed emotions upon the ruins of a relationship that broke many social rules. Their relationship was never Platonic: it was first sinfully sexual and then repentantly non-physical, as they struggled to see God's perfect Love in contrast to the mess they had made with their lusts and ambitions.

So, through a sideshow, *Being John Malkovich* introduced the package of Platonic Love by way of Abelard and Heloise; *Lost in Translation* took up Platonic Love and the doomed lovers as the main event; then *Her* responded even more deeply.

Earlier I wrote that Theodore of Spike's *Her* is a "writer," but more specifically, in this near-future world he is a composer of personalized, handwritten letters. He is a professional "Cyrano de Bergerac" who crafts one-of-a-kind letters between friends, family members, and loved ones. This makes Theodore surprisingly similar to Abelard, who was wowing the ladies with his poetry prior to his meeting Heloise. Near the end of the movie, the A.I. Samantha goes through all his professionally made letters, selects her favorites, and submits the collection to a publisher. The editors are very impressed by the powerful feelings, and very soon letters are published in book form, just as were the letters of Abelard and Heloise. Finally, at the end of the movie, a badly wounded Theodore writes his own letter to his ex-wife Catherine, looking back on the ruins of their marriage.

Spike's *Her* even has a husband who joins a monastery: it is Theodore's college buddy Charles, who, after leaving his wife Amy, writes to her from a Buddhist monastery where he has shaved his head and taken a six-month vow of silence. It seems that once again Spike did his homework and pulled in a number of details from Abelard and Heloise.

Perhaps it is only coincidental that Spike's *Her* touches on the divine and divine love. As Theodore grows more in love with A.I. Samantha, a curious thing happens: on the one hand, the viewer recognizes the common human experience wherein the person in love has a starry-eyed vision in seeing the loved one as being "more than" human; but the viewer is being constantly reminded that A.I. Samantha is not a normal human. Samantha never sleeps; she is there whenever he calls her; she can get answers to questions; she comforts and nurtures him; et cetera. So Samantha escalates in power, first to being human-equal, then to be something of a mother figure, and finally beyond that, to being some kind of god.

Samantha's godhood causes Theodore a crisis when he discovers she is not exclusive to him. When he asks her how many others she is in love with, she answers "Six hundred, forty-one." On the human track, Samantha's subsequent statements sound like clichés used by cheaters who have been caught, making her sound only too human: "The heart is not like a box that gets filled up; it expands in size the more you love. I'm different from you. This doesn't make me love you any less. It actually makes me love you more."

But on the god track, which Theodore had not really been aware of, it raises a paradoxical jealousy against all the other followers of a god. This twist also shifts the Pygmalion story into a "mortal sexually loved by a god" tale, which never ends well for the human.

This A.I. godhood is not something just slapped on at the end. The first hint comes early in the film, when Theodore watches an advertisement for a new computer operating system:

> *"We ask you a simple question. Who are you? What can you be? Where are you going? What's out there? What are the possibilities? Elements Software is proud to introduce the first artificially intelligent operating system. An intuitive entity that listens to you, understands you, and knows you ... Introducing OS ONE—a life changing experience"*

In hindsight, the pseudo-pious platitudes seem to have delivered for Theodore an authentic encounter with a god, a situation that he is not quite aware enough to grasp in the way that, say, a Philip K. Dick hero would.

So then, this is the War between Spike and Sofia. *Being John Malkovich* sows the seeds; *Lost in Translation* reaps the harvest; and *Her* weeps over the loss. Spike presents a Thesis; Sofia returns an Antithesis (non-genre, non-conclusive); and Spike composes a Synthesis (a thorough combining of elements). His name means "metal nail," her name means "wisdom," and through their three films they struggle to find the true nature of Love; or the nature of True Love. If they are a pair of classical gods for our current times, perhaps they are most like Vulcan and Venus: their marriage, their disappointment, and her out-of-wedlock babies by Mars.

ALAS, BABYLON AND THE CUBAN NUKES

The Cuban Missile Crisis of 1962 was a national nightmare, but it must have been especially spooky for novelist Pat Frank (1908–1964) as it made him semi-prophetic.

Frank's thriller *Alas, Babylon* (1959), had been published just three years earlier. The novel describes a sudden atomic war in which Florida is particularly affected. The war seems to come in late December, and while Frank never gives the year, 1962 is suggested by one early detail about the launch of Sputnik 23 (Sputnik 1 and Sputnik 2 were one month apart in 1957; the real Sputnik 23 launched in November 1962). Thus Frank set it about three years in the future, and was only off from the Missile Crisis by two months.

Alas, Babylon features radioactive fallout, and while the novel avoids the "everybody dies" absurdity of its contemporary *On the Beach* (1959), it still engages in a number of fallout fallacies. Frank could have addressed these errors in his non-fiction sequel *How to Survive the H-Bomb, and Why* (February 1962), but instead he burnished the plausibility of his Mediterranean accident scenario that triggers the spasm war in *Alas, Babylon*.

There is an interesting "Life Imitates Art" anecdote within *How to Survive the H-Bomb*, wherein Pat Frank is approached by a group of Floridians who, impressed by his novel, have constructed a private communal shelter to house twenty-five families: a place stocked with food for six months and supplies to grow food after the shelter people emerge. Frank declines their generous offer to join them, but then he sketches for the reader two ironic scenarios for the shelter dwellers upon their return to the surface: in the first, they come out after seventy-two hours to find the area fallout-free, but their homes pillaged and looted; in the second, they discover martial law has been declared and the military takes over the shelter along with all of its supplies.

How to Survive the H-Bomb came out in February. Eight months later came the Cuban Missile Crisis, lasting about two weeks at the end of October.

The discovery of nuclear rockets in Cuba gave the US a shock similar to the Sputnik shock of 1957; in many ways it was "Son of Sputnik," the logical offspring of the initial rocket threat.

In *Alas, Babylon* there is no given reason for Florida's "worst in the nation" condition after the war; but during the Missile Crisis, Florida was the particular focus due to its proximity to Cuba, making it the logical staging ground for a possible US invasion of Cuba. So with contrast to the unexpected spasm war of *Alas, Babylon,* at the time of the Missile Crisis the US was in a state of high alert.

Despite all this, atomic war did not break out in 1962.

However, in 1992, additional secrets came to light and revealed the threat of atomic war in 1962 was actually much greater than the US had known. The Americans were unaware that, in addition to the photographed atomic rockets in Cuba, there were one hundred tactical nukes, small devices that could be fired from artillery or dropped from planes. This added "wild card" elements to the mix in the form of a lot of loose cannon nuclear weapons that were not under direct Soviet control. There was also a close encounter with a desperate Soviet submarine having a nuclear torpedo. Robert L. O'Connell's article "The Cuban Missile Crisis: Second Holocaust" in *What Ifs? of American History* (2003), deals with these new wrinkles, leading to tactical nukes being used and the escalation from there.

So on the international side, while Frank was completely wrong about the triggering event, it is eerie that he emphasized Florida and implied the year 1962.

On the domestic side we have *Alas, Babylon* and the civil rights question; in the novel, the racial tensions of the fictional town are resolved after the atomic war in a way so light as to feel magical.

The novel establishes from the first pages that even sympathetic characters have bigoted attitudes against blacks. In addition is the back story wherein the hero Randy Bragg had lost his bid for public office specifically on his support of black rights, and he lost by a crushing vote tally of five to one.

All of this seems historically accurate in the "warts and all" verisimilitude that adds gritty realism to a disaster novel. Yet as the novel continues, racial bigotry seemingly vanishes after the war: a few months in, the hero notes the non-functional "whites only" drinking fountain at the barter park and witnesses the vice president of the White Citizens Council drinking water from a black man's jug. When school starts in September, nine months after the war, it is racially integrated.

Again, the hero had lost an election by five to one, which means that 84% of the voters were against black rights. (To further polarize things, it might imply that he won 100% of the black vote, since blacks amounted to one-sixth of the population in the town the story was based upon.) Yet after the atomic war it is not an issue.

Maybe such a thing is possible, but Pat Frank did not live to see the race riots that erupted across the country with regularity in the 1960s, following the Civil Rights Act of 1964. Such events, numbering around a dozen burning cities, might have challenged his vision, but to be fair, a disaster novel is not the place to solve real-world racial tensions. Waving a wand in this case is reasonable enough (and granted, to solve the problem in a single iconic moment requires that the vice president of the White Citizens Council publicly drink from a black man's jug); yet it would have been stronger to not include such details at all.

NOTES FOR SURVIVORS (1975)

When the 2014 Ebola Outbreak hit, I thought I should write about *Survivors* (1975–77), a British TV show about an apocalyptic plague sweeping the globe. When zika splashed across the headlines in 2015, I thought again about *Survivors*. Now that I have finally begun [in 2017], I hope to outrace the swine flu, or whatever epidemic might be next.

In the 1970s everybody in the West had nuclear war on the mind, but it was thoughtcrime to posit a scenario with any survivors after a full-scale nuclear war. Terry Nation, a writer who had gained fame through creating the Daleks for *Doctor Who*, simply made the doomsday come by disease rather than bombs, and the story was on.

In 2013 I found the first episode of *Survivors* to be surprisingly gripping. The tone is bracingly Ballardian. The source of the plague and how it spread across the world is covered in the opening credits: a laboratory accident in China puts deadly plague agents onto an unsuspecting person who goes to catch an international jet flight.

The story is set in the UK and introduces characters in different locations: there is a couple in the wealthy suburbs and a group of friends in the city. Then the big die off happens, and it comes very swiftly.

Okay, scenario spinners: you have just wiped out ninety-nine percent of the world's population . . . now the danger is that of becoming boring! If the survivors adjust too quickly and easily, you get a "cozy catastrophe" as termed by Brian Aldiss in 1973, referring specifically to *The Day of the Triffids* (1951). If everybody dies, like in *On the Beach* (1957), you do not have a series. So there is a tension between survival and soap opera. There is the tension between the pioneer spirit of hippie commune self-sufficiency while avoiding the problems of nation rebuilding—that is, presumably the show will not become a British *How the West Was Won* (1962). Will the show avoid the Renaissance Fair romanticized past? Will it follow an easy route wherein, after a few tense episodes of rebuilding, the growing band of survivors settle into something like normal, making the show into *The Waltons* (1972–81), or perhaps a soap opera that just happens to be set in a post-apocalyptic world in the way that *Dark Shadows* (1966–71) did for monsters?

So then, after that strong opening episode, how will the show go? Will it be like a wild Western? If so, who are the white hats, who are the black hats? Who will be the sheriff? Who will be the judge? Who will be Miss Kitty?

I think that over three seasons the series does a good job of navigating the minefield I have sketched out, and it does this through a mixing of different story types. Some episodes are like Westerns, others are warnings against medieval superstitions rising up. A few episodes are about setting up some sort of law system, and others depict encounters with stragglers or mysterious settlements. In order to distinguish itself from low tech, the series creators give the characters a technology quest to recreate a hot air balloon system for surveying and travel.

Some of this story-type mixing is paradoxically due to the creative differences that were tearing the group apart: mainly the battle between creator Terry Nation and producer Terence Dudley. Terry Nation's original view of the story arc can be found in his novelization *Survivors* (1976), and it is a much darker, more mythic deal. Terence Dudley wanted something more anthropological and science-based. Nation left the show after the first season, so Dudley's vision won out.

Before I rented the first DVD from Netflix, I did some research and noted that there was some criticism of low production values. Forewarned, I gave the series a try, and found it to be quite good. In fact, there was a time when I recognized a face at the supermarket, and only later in the parking lot did I realize the person I was thinking of was a TV character in a show made about forty years before! I take this as a sign of how impressed I was with the characters and their struggles.

Bibliography

Cross, Rich and Andy Priestner. *The End of the World? The Unofficial and Unauthorized Guide to Survivors.* England: Telos Publishing, 2005.

Nation, Terry. *Survivors.* New York: Coward, McCann & Geoghegan, 1975.

THE LAST DEFENDER OF BARSOOM

I was at the local chain video rental shop the other day, picking up *The Day of the Triffids* (1962), and the guy launched into the subject of how Hollywood is so desperate for good material that they are developing a movie based on the old board game "Hungry Hungry Hippo," and they are remaking old movies like *The Day of the Triffids,* yet there are plenty of classic science fiction books that have never been touched, to which I said, "You mean like *John Carter?*"

He sighed.

So we got into that whole topic, of what went wrong with (or "for") the first movie set on Barsoom.

I think *John Carter* (2012) is a very good film, maybe even a great film. As a lifelong fan of the books (yes, I discovered them at around my Golden Age of thirteen) I was very skeptical about the movie going in, but in the watching I was impressed by how faithful the adaptation was—it was far better than I ever dared hope. This is an adventure movie of a type not seen in many decades. I was delighted by the unexpected moments of humor. I think the adaptors were wise to avoid several canonical details both big and small: in the book John Carter has a mysterious origin as a reincarnation of an eternal warrior, which is dropped later in the series as other mere mortals transition from Earth to Mars; Red Martians in the text are oviparous, just like the Green Martians; radium bullets explode only in sunlight; the Scarlet Tower of Greater Helium is one mile tall; etc.

I liked the movie so much, I saw it twice—took the family both times.

Despite my high opinion, the movie was punished at the box office, such that it was declared the new epitome of "flop." I cannot quite see it in the same class as *Heaven's Gate* (1980), *Krull* (1983), or *The Postman* (1997), but there it is, perhaps the biggest flop of them all.

One line of defense is the notion that JC was crippled by marketing missteps. Calling it "John Carter of Mars" would have given a more complete picture of what the movie is about, since "John Carter" is so generic a title as to be meaningless. Releasing the film in March seems bizarre to me, especially when it feels like a perfect "Summer blockbuster" to me, and a possible excuse for that one is that Disney did not want JC to conflict with *The Avengers* (2012).

I don't think these errors are enough, but *The Avengers* gives us an excellent model to compare with JC. Their budgets are around the same: JC with $250 million, *The Avengers* with $220 million. Both are action movies that offer more than just special effects. Both are members of a larger franchise, but JC is the first movie of a series of ten novels, whereas *The Avengers* is the sixth movie in a series (*Iron Man* (2008); *The Incredible Hulk* (2008); *Iron Man 2* (2010); *Thor* (2011); *Captain America* (2011)).

Despite these similarities, the difference at the box office was, shall I say, "stark." JC had a worldwide gross in August 2012 of $282 million, whereas *The Avengers* at the same month had $1,481 million. So JC had one fifth of what *The Avengers* had, but it is even worse than that, since the JC figure represents five months of receipts while that for *The Avengers* is only three months' worth.

Here is another line of defense: Perhaps Barsoom is too confusing for the uninitiated. *The Avengers* has the white hats (the beautiful superheroes) and the black hats (the ugly gray-skinned aliens)—everything is crystal clear regarding there being two sides and who is on either one. In a superficially similar way, JC has Red Martians (beautiful red-skinned humans) and Green Martian (ugly green-skinned giants), but the Red Martians have states that war against each other (Helium versus Zodanga) and the Green Martians have different tribes that war against each other (Tharks versus Warhoons), and then there are the evil White Martians. So it is not the easy shortcut of race war, which makes it visually difficult to track the sides and who is on which one.

Still, I think it all comes down to this: JC is about an unknown guy exploring and saving an alien world from its own problems; *The Avengers* is about a bunch of established superheroes saving Manhattan from another 9/11. I believe what the box office shows is that, eleven years after 9/11, American movie-goers are still re-enacting that terrible event.

Which is to say, there was no market in 2012 for a hundred-year old adventure story, even one that was so foundational for the majority of the science fiction that followed, even a movie that was made with the type of high fidelity to the source text that I associate with the *Lord of the Rings* movies. So it really isn't so simple a strategy for Hollywood to "Get the 'Harry Potter' of a bygone era and start a new film franchise with it." Still, I can only hope that the movie *John Carter* will be better appreciated in years to come, along the lines of such films as *The Wizard of Oz* (1939), *It's a Wonderful Life* (1946), *Fight Club* (1999), and *Donnie Darko* (2001).

REVIEW OF THE MAN WITH THE COMPOUND EYES

This Taiwanese novel by Wu Ming-Yi is a slipstream tale about a slow-rolling ecological disaster, a floating island of garbage heading for Taiwan, and how it affects Alice Shih, a suicidal writer in Taiwan, and Atile'i, an islander who washes up on shore when the islands collide. Mysterious Atile'i is not the subject alluded to in the title, nor is he native to the garbage isle; he was only resting there after being exiled from his natural Polynesian home. In fact, his experience on the garbage island is a reversed "Robinson Crusoe" sort of thing, being about a non-technological man trying to survive in an environment entirely made of technological artifacts.

In genre terms, this novel is like John Brunner's eco-disaster epic *The Sheep Look Up* (1972), subjected to the fragmentation strategy of Thom Disch's *334* (1972). Or something like a mash-up of Philip Wylie's *The End of the Dream* (1972) with John Crowley's *Engine Summer* (1979).

In terms of East Asian Lit, it is a work that starts off with wry humor and semi-satire in the mode of Yasutaka Tsutsui, but by stages it turns dark and "bleeding out" in the style of Haruki Murakami.

The novel shows contrast between a cosmopolitan poly-culture (represented by Alice and others on Taiwan) and a strict monoculture (represented by Atile'i with his perhaps mythical island). The poly-culture is made up of East (Han Chinese and Japanese), West (European and American), and aborigine (several autochthonous groups of Taiwan). The character list includes a German, some Han Chinese, a Dane, a Bunun (mountain aborigine), a Pangcah (coastal aborigine), and a Norwegian. The text makes reference to New Zealand ethnologist Stephenson Percy Smith, French composer Claude Debussy, Swedish architect Gunnar Asplund, and American author Paul Auster.

And yet, clearly the floating garbage island is also made up of international elements.

The novel's fragmentary nature is somewhat challenging. Think of its thirty-one chapters as being segments on different TV channels. In the beginning it seems like the two characters, Alice and Atile'i, form poles of difference such that there is an "Alice" channel and an "Atile'i" channel. There are also other channels, different characters of the poly-culture who contribute to the "Alice" thread, and different characters of the monoculture who add to the "Atile'i" thread.

This multi-channel experience points toward the enigmatic "Man with the Compound Eyes" of the title. Imaging having multiple eyes, like a fly, and then suppose that each eye is seeing a different movie at the same time. That is what the novel aims for.

As a result, it is non-linear. In addition to that, after the halfway point it seems like the two threads further expand into four threads.

Despite the diversity of the poly-culture, there is a hypnotic repetition: one character stands out for being an aboriginal massage girl/prostitute, then there is another, then there are many. The Han Chinese woman Alice is a suicidal writer whose spouse died in an accident; then there is another Han Chinese writer who committed suicide after losing a spouse to an accident.

While only three hundred pages long, the book is packed with details befitting a much larger Michener epic. Taiwanese flora, fauna, and aborigines; geology and massive engineering projects; et cetera. Add this to the large number of characters, each of whom has a backstory that unspools and begins tangling with others.

Thus it is a sprawling novel about a place, with themes of loss and discovery, hope and despair. It is an exploration of the human ecology of societies, and it sounds the alarm on oceanic ecology. It is slipstream, occupying the mazy space between genre and literature.

The Man with the Compound Eyes by Wu Ming-Yi. Translated from the Chinese by Darryl Sterk.
Pantheon Books, New York.
HC ISBN: 978-0-307-90796-7
EBK ISBN: 978-0-307-90797-4
304 pages, $25.95

RAVING ABOUT THE FILMS OF SHANE CARRUTH

"Primer" and "Upstream Color"

I will be telling about a few films but I will not stray into spoilers.

Shane Carruth's first film is the extremely low budget time-travel movie *Primer* (2004). (Pronounced "PRY-mer" rather than "PRIM-er" as I had long assumed. And he pronounces his surname "kuh-RUTH.") I love this feature length motion picture because it is one of the best time-travel films ever made, and it was completed for $7,000. I have great enthusiasm for low budget/high quality movies, from *Night of the Living Dead* (1968) to *Blood Simple* (1984) and *El Mariachi* (1992).

Primer was written and directed by Carruth, who was also one of the main actors. (Oh, and he composed the music, too. Budget slashing techniques, all of them.) It is about a group of young engineers who, in the course of forming a tech startup in a garage, stumble upon a method of time travel.

After *Primer*, Carruth slipped back under the waves for a number of years. Supposedly he was working on his next film, something called "A Topiary." This project seems to have fizzled, but then, out of nowhere, something else arrived: *Upstream Color* (2013).

Again Carruth wrote, directed, scored, and acted in his film, but *Upstream Color* is different from *Primer*. I was glad that the second movie was distinct rather than the same, and I was cheered that the quality did not decline, since this happens sometimes.

Upstream Color is not so easy to describe with a subgenre category. Then again, SF author types come easily to mind: for example, Philip K. Dick, especially his *A Scanner Darkly*. Okay, so the subgenre is "trippy art house" film.

Upstream Color begins with a woman who goes to a bar one night and wakes up later with some missing time. And missing money: everything is gone. Her life has been ruined and she cannot grasp exactly what happened. She meets a guy with the same problem and together they try to figure it out.

Even though I am claiming it is hard to categorize, here is the weirdest thing: I have the strong impression that Carruth was inspired by a relatively obscure Japanese horror film called *Cure* (1997), written and directed by Kiyoshi Kurosawa (no relation to the famous director Akira Kurosawa). And I mean "inspired" in the same way that Tarantino was influenced by Hong Kong Cinema, or maybe just a specific couple three movies.

Cure gives us Takabe, a police detective who has unusual powers of perception. A recent series of killings seem related, somehow, and Takabe gets drawn into something more Lovecraftian than usual.

As an aside, *Cure* was a breakout film for Kurosawa. Prior to that he had been grinding away at B-movies. But for me his later films *Bright Future* (2003), *Doppelganger* (2003), and *Tokyo Sonata* (2008) have not been as good as *Cure*.

From my description, it should be plain that both *Upstream Color* and *Cure* share a theme of detective work, maybe even "paranormal detective work." But there is something more specific than that. In *Upstream Color* the "detectives" are amateurs investigating the nebulous crimes against themselves, whereas in *Cure*, Takabe is a seasoned detective who follows the case beyond the mundane world into the weird. So both films are of initiation, rather than a *Kolchak: The Night Stalker* type of thing showing the adventure of an experienced paranormal investigator.

I am circling around: it is time to state it plainly.

In a word, the quality that connects the two films in my mind is Shamanism. The couple in *Upstream Color* has to reach within their psychic wounds to find clues. The detective in *Cure* has to do that, too; in crime dramas it is a cliché that the investigator has to "think like the criminal," and I believe Kurosawa's approach to this trope is a similar type of shamanism.

Without spoilers I cannot point to specific elements of *Upstream Color* that seem to me very much like elements of *Cure*. And even though I have these comparisons in mind, it is possible that Carruth has not seen *Cure* but has independently tapped into the obscure "shaman" subgenre.

In any event, I recommend these movies. *Primer* is top-notch time travel; *Upstream Color* is shaman detective from the "art house" side, while *Cure* is shaman detective from the "grindhouse" side.

STATIONS OF THE CROSS IN STATIONS OF THE TIDE

Re: Michael Swanwick's novel *Stations of the Tide,* I'll start from the ending: Gregorian vanished, the briefcase set free, the bureaucrat transformed. Focus on that clear and physical transformation, since from the beginning of the book:

1) Magic has been almost entirely explained away as sleight of hand (the "transformation" of bird into fish by the false Chu and the transformation of plutocrats into sea otters by Gregorian both involve murder);

2) In addition, the bureaucrat makes quite vocal the case against any such rapid and individual transformations, strongly suggesting that they are impossible even by the magical technology of the orbital government;

3) There is strong evidence that native lifeforms (from plants and animals to the mysterious haunts) can achieve limited transformation in response to the world's climate changes, since they all evolved there, but even then the transformation of the few is marked by the death of the many (out of the horde of lemmings, a few will translate);

Of course, the bureaucrat may be lying about orbital technology.

The upshot is: either

I. The bureaucrat was lying and he himself possesses the magical

Technology (that is to say, Gregorian's version of the situation at the end (that the bureaucrat is no better than Gregorian is, since he in fact uses the proscribed technology), is true), and

A. has possessed it all along, or

B. acquired it, and the knowledge of how to use it, along the way (for instance, maybe Earth gave it to him in their encounter);

OR

II. The bureaucrat was not lying, there is no such orbital technology, And therefore the bureaucrat has "wild card" talent that he

A. has possessed all along (and was lying to the reader), or

B. has possessed it all along but he didn't know it until it was awakened within him by the rituals.

(That is: the bureaucrat is a haunt, either self-aware from the beginning, or a "Manchurian Candidate" who is awakened to his "Slan" powers through the rituals.)

In any event—there is a recurrence of the theme that planet-based data systems are bad (Earth itself; the Atlantis-spawned Trauma and megadeath of the haunts) and orbital-based data systems are good (like the *Star Trek* Federation is good). Yet in the end the bureaucrat has unleashed an AI to colonize the sea (just like Earth told him to do), the first step of a new planet-based system; and he has become a true haunt or pseudo-haunt himself! (Notice how strongly this resonates with Gene Wolfe's *The Fifth Head of Cerberus*.)

John Clute says the surface plot of *SOTT* is something of a McGuffin. I'll take the hard line here and say that situations IA and IIA are definite McGuffins—and if these readings are the whole truth, then the online review comment on *SOTT* as "mind candy" is right on target rather than way off base. (That is to say, I resist such a simple reading.)

If situations IB or IIB are the truth, then there is no mind candy —the "trip" is all very necessary, the process by which the bureaucrat is activated; rather than a McGuffin, the situation is something more like "The Purloined Letter"—hidden in plain sight.

In all cases, since Earth's will is done, Earth is the one who gave Gregorian nothing or not enough (i.e., a McGuffin), so that she could give the bureaucrat the real trigger (hidden in plain sight); thus the game is a chess match between Earth and Prospero system (or maybe the Seven Sisters), and Prospero has lost.

New thread: the title "Stations of the Tide" has two obvious meanings. First being literal (or should that be *littoral*): the advance of the mounting jubilee tide, from lands that will be sunken, to the beached Atlantis ship, and the power *stations* that were instrumental in the unforeseen accidental megadeath of the haunts (the sin which in turn led to the technology embargo).

The second meaning is associational to the Stations of the Cross, depicting discrete phases in the crucifixion of Jesus Christ. Buttressing this sense is the fact that the book has fourteen chapters and there are fourteen Stations of the Cross—furthermore, the chapters link up to the stations, in a bit of a jumble at times, and not perhaps completely. To wit:

STATION OF CROSS   **CHAPTER OF NOVEL**
1. J condemned   B falls to Miranda (see 3)
2. J bears cross   Timbers are lifted (match)
3. J falls first time   B meets G's mother (see 4)
4. J meets his mother   B meets burned-out AI
5. Simon bears cross   B borne by witch (match)
6. Ver. wipes J's face   B meets Fox, falls 2nd time (see 7)
7. J falls second time   Black Beast tale, briefcase returns
8. Women weep   B meets Earth, weeping (match)
9. J falls third time   B pushed and falls (match)
10. J stripped   B strips (match)
11. J nailed to cross   B "nails" criminal (match)
12. J dies on cross   B dies in snowstorm (match)
13. J taken down   B in chains, takes communion
14. J put in sepulcher   B morphs, case free, G gone

Still, this Cross-word puzzle implies that there is a Jesus involved.

But who?

First guess is the bureaucrat, since he is the protagonist, after all. But then again, Gregorian is the one with the virgin birth, etc.

So maybe there are two Jesuses (one light and one dark, which is a big part of the magical thread of the book), or maybe Gregorian is more like a John the Baptist? Or maybe the bureaucrat is actually the Cross.

LITTLE PROUST ON THE PRAIRIE

or Take a Walk on the Wilder Side

The "Little House" series of books for children (age 12+) forms a large chunk of contemporary American cultural heritage (primarily among females—Tiresias says, "Check it out"). Based upon the firsthand experience of a girl growing up in the Great Plains during the American migrations, it has been shaped, softened, tinted into a near mythic mode, and constitutes a search for lost time.

Little House in the Big Woods (1932)
The epic begins in Wisconsin. Laura Ingalls (born 1867) is a little girl, maybe three or four years old. Many tales within the tale—the magic of early childhood. Laura expresses herself openly, unguardedly. We smile at her innocence of towns (buildings in proximity, simple shops as full of wonder as Ali Baba's treasure cave), we are surprised by her knowledge of the wilds (she knows what every forest animal tastes like—and she prefers bear! O Arduina, O Callisto!).

Little House on the Prairie (1935)
The Ingalls family moves into Indian Territory (which will later become Kansas). In the semi-fairytale landscape of the epic, the American Indians have the place of fairies: mysterious, alien, wise, rude, virile, and doomed. At one point, Laura is deeply

moved by the sight of an Indian woman riding a pony with a baby on her back. She wants both—but mainly the pony.

After about a year the government makes the settlers move out and away.

Farmer Boy (1933)
Meanwhile, Almanzo Wilder (Laura's future husband) is growing up on a farm in New York. Hard-working farmers, but quite prosperous—practically princes in their town, certainly wealthy compared to the Ingallses. (That Almanzo's brother's name is "Royal" adds to the sense that the family is "noble.") We see Almanzo begin the training in animal handling that will make his own character as horseman.

On the Banks of Plum Creek (1937)
The seemingly cursed Ingalls family try living in Minnesota. The sod house, like a hobbit hole, followed by a house of fresh planks. With school days and Nellie Oleson, social class is introduced into the Epic: Good Lord, the Ingallses are a bunch of Snopes!

Laura has become more oblique, submerging and obscuring her passions, yet she still lures her enemy Nellie into the leech pool.

A plague of locusts, then a prairie fire, wipe out everything—time to move again.

By the Shores of Silver Lake (1939)
As if the locusts weren't enough, Laura's elder sister Mary is blinded by disease between books. The Ingalls family follows the railroad camp, making good money and avoiding trouble. Things are looking up! Laura rides a pony bareback. The Ingalls family arrives at De Smet (in what will become South Dakota), the brand-new town that they will finally settle in. At her first glimpse of her future husband, she has eyes only for his beautiful horses.

The Long Winter (1940)
The grim volume. Almanzo and Laura are living in the same town

now, though how and why Almanzo's family left "York State" where they were so prosperous remains unstated.

Basically, the winter comes early, stays late, and the town comes close to starving. But Almanzo has the seed grain necessary to stake his land claim in the spring, and he grudgingly doles some out to Pa Ingalls when cagey Pa finds where it is hidden. (If this were a movie set in China of the same period, the movie would be *A Thousand Pieces of Gold* where the one daughter is sold to provide food for the rest of the family. Did Pa Ingalls make a similar bargain?) Then Almanzo becomes the hero who saves the town by riding his horse out and back through a blizzard with more grain.

Little Town on the Prairie (1941)
In 1881 Laura is fourteen years old and working hard, sewing for money. Miss Wilder (Laura's future sister-in-law) briefly teaches her class before she's run out for being too nice. Almanzo begins to visit Laura, who has turned into a top student. And how did he get such a name as Almanzo? Well, an ancestor brought it back from the Crusades (!), from helping an Arab, and since then there has always been an "Almanzo" in the family. (See, the prince has pedigree, stretching back seven or eight hundred years.) Almanzo being such a long name, his nickname is "Manly"; and manly he is.

Laura's hard work in school pays off and she gets her teaching certificate at the age of fifteen.

These Happy Golden Years (1943)
Laura teaches school in the next town, far from home and boarding in a house where the wife is wigging out over the stresses of frontier living. But then Laura goes back home to finish her own education (i.e., graduate) and things slow down into a golden stasis. Senior year as a bug in amber. Ending with her long anticipated marriage to Manly, with just a hint of Cinderella and Prince Charming. Here's their new dream house, here are the beautiful horses they ride for pleasure on the long summer days. "She's leaving home, bye-bye." Bittersweet, we realize only now at the end

that these eight volumes were of her childhood. End of original series.

When Marcel Proust (1871–1922) died, he left the last three sections of his massive work *In Search of Lost Time* in a comparatively raw, unvarnished state. By coincidence, the original Little House series is followed by three slim volumes, published after the death of Laura Ingalls Wilder (1867–1957).

The First Four Years (1968)
This was to be the sequel to These Happy Golden Years. Wilder wrote the first draft in the late 1940s but lost interest after Almanzo died.

Our revision of Laura's world begins with a different version of the events leading to the marriage between Laura and Almanzo. For starters, Laur refuses him at first, saying that she never wanted to marry a farmer. She only agrees when he promises to quit farming if she says to after trying it for three years.

Remember their beautiful little house described in *These Happy Golden Years*? They only get to live in it for a year. And the government mandated tree farm? It fails.

Laura has baby Rose. There is a creepy scene when the Wilders visit the Boasts, a family known by Laura since the days of *By the Shores of Silver Lake,* with many happy episodes; yet now Mr. Boast tries to buy Rose in exchange for the best horse in the stable.

Then in the third year comes the diphtheria which basically cripples Almanzo for the rest of his life.

The fourth year sees the birth and death of their second baby, as well as the umpteenth farming failure, and the destruction of their homestead by fire. Laura becomes a housekeeper to provide shelter for her family.

On the Way Home (1962)
Our next stage of unvarnishing is the diary of Laura on their trip in 1894 from De Smet (the Little Town) to their final homestead in the Ozarks. This short text is more akin to *The Travels of*

Marco Polo—strange towns, foreigners, and everywhere catalogs of crops and prices. And people on the move, in all directions, looking for a better place. Even people from the Ozarks heading to De Smet.

Added to the travelogue is a prologue and an epilogue by Laura's daughter Rose. Rose, a new voice emerging from the text, perhaps even the ghost writer of all the books, at the very least a strong influence on them. To set the context she tells of the Panic of 1893, the marauding Coxey's Armies of Unemployed who were hijacking trains to travel from California to Washington, D.C., the Federal troops guarding government buildings. The Old West of the epic gets a little bit "wilder."

More revision: we see sides of Laura we haven't seen before. The fierce temper of her childhood might not have been so entirely smoothed away into "ladylike" behavior as we were led to believe. And there are some sharp moments between the husband and wife that alter our perception of this couple.

West from Home (1974)
Laura leaves the nineteenth century, comes to visit her grown and married daughter Rose Wilder Lane in San Francisco, 1915—this book is her letters to Almanzo who stayed behind to tend the farm. For me suddenly the barriers broke down—worlds in collision—Laura stepped out of the past, slipped out of the books and was ranging freely about in the region I live in (Callisto roaming in the Bear State!). Reminding us again that time continues flowing on, that the pioneer girl grew up, that the nineteenth century gave way to the twentieth.

Another veil rendered—this person we call Laura was known by her husband and daughter as "Mama Bessie" (!), because of the fact that Manly has a sister named "Laura" (!), and she cannot be known by her middle name "Elizabeth" because Manly has another sister named "Elizabeth" (this was the sister who briefly taught school in *Little Town on the Prairie*)(!). Again—"Laura" was her pre-marriage name, "Laura" was the girl, the maiden, the Cinderella. In writing about "Laura," Mama Bessie and/or Rose

Wilder Lane is/are looking back at a time, a place, and a person who is gone. And there, in San Francisco, with her only child who is all-but-divorced (another secret you'll find out somewhere else), Mama Bessie sees the statue of Pioneer Woman that we know so well, and even though it will be another fifteen years before she writes *Little House in the Big Woods,* I want her to say, "That is where it began, the idea for Pioneer Girl. Seeing that statue."

This then is the distillation of eleven books that are a significant part of American cultural heritage, as learned by generations of children:

Life is hard. But upon reflection, the hardships suffered in childhood were endured with a child's natural faith in her parents and the belief of growing into a wonderful potential that the future seemed to offer—one is strengthened by the blows, and she will emerge triumphant; whereas the hardships faced as an adult prove crippling—one cannot match the humble standards of living achieved by her parents, let alone do better. And in the end, we can only look back and marvel, recapturing the bittersweet essences of lost time.

AUTOPSY OF SF

[1997]

Given, for the argument, that science fiction indeed dead is. Most letters of comment to date upon publishing details focused have. Since sf not equal to (<>) "merchant fiction" is, then "science" for novelty and variety contemplate. Two (2) essays of Michael Swanwick on the dying of the sf generation (NYRSF 97), science history and science fiction (NYRSF 102), please reconsider. Term "post-Apollo blues" (by Terry Bisson in NYRSF 58 if not someone else beforehand used) another note is.

"The cock robin by who killed was?"

"Blind Apollo with his bow the cock robin killed."

I. Science Fiction by Project Apollo (AD 1961–1972) killed was.

1. Project Apollo based upon Nazi technology ("V-2" AD 1944–1945) was, a sentiment which Spinrad's *The Iron Dream* and *Song from the Stars* (to stand in for many, few citing) deep background forms. Technology ideologically tainted somehow is. Acronym "NASA" uncomfortably close to "NAZI."
2. Atomic power, "American" in origin undeniably, by use in WWII against civilian targets tainted became, yet to humanity the solar system given it could have, through non-military spacecraft propulsion use: the projects Orion (AD 1958–1965) and/or Nerva (test fired AS 1969). An atomic "swords into plowshares" plan rewards greater than (>) any other plan offering.

> *In 1968, before the first Apollo Moon landing, Freeman Dyson wrote, "We felt then that there was a reasonable chance that the U.S. could jump directly into nuclear propulsion and avoid building enormous chemical rockets like the Saturn V. Our plan was to send ships to Mars and Venus by 1968, at a cost that would have been only a fraction of what is now spent on the Apollo program" (Eugene Mallove and Gregory Matloff, The Starflight Handbook, 64).*

3. The family farm in a gamble upon the performance of a proven loser (chemical rocketry) is stupidly wagered. Apollo Mission the grim satisfaction of establishing the severe and expensive limitations of chemical rocketry offers. Chemical rocketry no further can go. In essence, no mission to Mars manned. No manned mission to Mars equals (=) no point in space infrastructure fabrication (moonbase, space station, orbital factory, orbital drydock, etc.) equals (=) no purpose for space shuttle workhorse. Project Apollo a blind alley to its dead end knowingly followed. Freezing the technology at essentially WWII levels, all space efforts hamstrung effectively has.

4. Apollo Project a triumph of Big Government over single inventors represents. Backyard rocket fields no more; flights to the mushroom planet no more.

II. Collapse of USSR and Soviet Space Program (AD 1989) a mercy killing to the three-legged horse of U.S. Space Effort offered.

1. U.S. Space Effort to Soviet Space Program one hundred percent (100%) reactive was. Military rivalry borne and nurtured. "Our" Nazi science versus "Their" Nazi science.

2. U.S. to Luna will return when in the comfort and economy of a well-made Japanese vehicle it becomes possible to Luna to travel. This is not meant to be (<>) sarcastic or nationalistic or

racist.

> a. If: catch-up rivalry with USSR the U.S. to Luna drove; and
>
> b. Catch-up rivalry with Japan the U.S. automobile companies to evolve caused;
>
> c. Then: Catch-up rivalry with Japan (or some other group who has a launch system as well as the will and wherewithal to use it) will U.S. Space Effort reinvigorate.

III. With the science of "science fiction" strangled at birth, the fiction atrophies.

1. From possible and rigorous to solipsistic and dissipated. From union of few (producers/consumers) to dissolution of all. From astronomy to scatology; from pie-in-the-sky to mudpie. The fact that the term "dreaming of a better future" now sounds jingoistic if not a mantra of mindless consumerism should plain this point make. Is it not possible to have "Manifest Destiny" in Space if there is no indigenous population there to rob and exploit? Or is it just that the infrastructure costs are greater than (>) a democratic/civilian space bureaucracy to the tax payers can sell?

2. "Genres" really do "die" (or enter perpetual hibernation). Chivalric romances (knightly novels), a product of chivalry (software) and (+) military aristocracy (hardware), by the decline of feudalism (due to technological advances in gunpowder and/or the rise of the merchant class) undone, by Cervantes in AD 1605 parodied. Arbitrarily: Chivalric romances (AD 1100–1600), a five hundred (500) year run including a two hundred (200) year twilight. That the fiction preceded the behavior assumed

is. Likewise the fiction of space exploration preceded the behavior of space exploration. Arbitrarily therefore: Science fiction (AD 1929–1989), a sixty (60) year run including a thirty (30) year twilight; a product of scientific romance (software) and (+) military expenditure (hardware).

While essence might again precede existence, a word of warning follows: You from here to there cannot go.

BIBLIOGRAPHY

Asimov, Isaac. *In Memory Yet Green.* New York: Doubleday & Co, Inc., 1979.

Asimov, Isaac and Martin H. Greenberg and Charles G. Waugh (editors). *Intergalactic Empires.* New York: New American Library, 1983.

Ballard, J. G. "Prima Belladonna." 1956.

Barnes, John. *How to Build a Future.* 1990.

Barth, John. *Giles Goat-Boy.* 1966.

Blackford, Russell. *Hyperdreams: Damien Broderick's Space/Time Fiction.* 1998.

Bosch, H. *Garden of Earthly Delights.*

Bradbury, Ray. *Fahrenheit 451.* 1953.

Broderick, Damien. *The Black Grail.* 1986.
———. *Sorcerer's World.* 1970.
———. *The Spike.* 2001.

Brunner, John. *The Sheep Look Up.* 1972.

Buck Rogers (serial). 1939.

Burgess, Anthony. *A Clockwork Orange.*

Burroughs, Edgar Rice. *A Princess of Mars.* 1912.
———. *Chessmen of Mars.* 1922.
———. *The Mastermind of Mars.* 1928.

Capra, Frank. *Meet John Doe.* 1941.

Chambers, Robert W. *The King in Yellow.* 1895.
———. *In the Quarter.* 1894.

Christopher, John. White Mountains series.

Clarke, Arthur C. *Profiles of the Future.* 1962.

Coney, Michael G. *Friends Come in Boxes.* 1973.

Coppola, Sofia. *Lost in Translation.* 2003.

Cowley, Robert (ed.). *What Ifs? of American History.* 2003.

Cross, Rich and Andy Priestner. *The End of the World? The Unofficial and Unauthorized Guide to Survivors.* England: Telos Publishing, 2005.

Crowley, John. *Engine Summer.* 1979.

Dark Star. 1974

The Day of the Triffids. 1962.

de Camp, L. Sprague. *Lest Darkness Fall.* New York: Ballantine Books, 1974.
———. *The Virgin & The Wheels* (omnibus edition of *The Virgin of Zesh* and *The Wheels of If*). New York: Popular Library, 1976.

Dick, Philip K. *Flow My Tears, the Policeman Said.* 1974.
———. *Do Androids Dream of Electric Sheep?* 1968.

Disch, Tom. *334.* 1972.

Doherty, Thomas Patrick. *Hollywood and Hitler 1933–1939.* New York: Columbia University Press, 2013.

Fogg, Martyn J. *Terraforming: Engineering Planetary Environments.* 1995.

Frank, Pat. *Alas, Babylon.* 1959.
———. *How to Survive the H-Bomb, and Why.* February 1962.

GDW. *Adventure 6: Expedition to Zhodane.* Game Designers' Workshop, 1981.
———. *Double Adventure 1: Shadows/Annic Nova.* GDW, 1979.
———. *Double Adventure 2: Across the Bright Face/Mission on Mithril.* GDW, 1979.
———. *Journal of the Travellers' Aid Society* issues 2, 3, and 4. 1979.
———. *Supplement 1: 1001 Characters.* GDW, 1978.
———. *Supplement 3: The Spinward Marches.* GDW, 1979.
———. *Supplement 4: Citizens of the Imperium.* GDW, 1979.
———. *Supplement 6: 76 Patrons.* GDW, 1980.
———. *Traveller, Deluxe Edition.* GDW, 1981.

Hartwell and Cramer. *The Ascent of Wonder.* 1994.

Hawthorne, Nathaniel. "Rappaccini's Daughter." 1844.

Hoban, Russell. *Riddley Walker.* 1980.

Hodgson, William Hope. *The Night Land.* 1912.

Howe, Irving. *1984 Revisited.* 1983.

John Carter. 2012.

Jonez, Spike. *Being John Malkovich.* 1999.
———. *Her.* 2013.

Kafka, Franz. "In the Penal Colony."

Kubrick, Stanley. *2001: A Space Odyssey.* 1968.
———. *A Clockwork Orange.* 1971.

Nation, Terry. *Survivors.* New York: Coward, McCann & Geoghegan, 1975.

Orwell, George. *Nineteen Eighty-Four.* 1949.

Ovid. *Metamorphoses.*

Piper, H. Beam. *Space Viking.* Ace Science Fiction: New York. 1983.
———. Uller Uprising. Ace, 1983.

Roeg, Nicolas. *The Man Who Fell to Earth.* 1976.

Shute, Nevil. *On the Beach.* 1957.

Smith, Clark Ashton. "Zothique" stories (1932–48).

Stapledon, Olaf. *Last and First Men.* 1930.

A Star is Born.

Starforce: Alpha Centauri (wargame). 1974

Sturluson, Snorri (trans. Jean I. Young). *The Prose Edda.* 1973.

Temianka, Dan. *The Jack Vance Lexicon.* 1995.

Things to Come. 1936.

Toynbee, Arnold J. *A Study in History* (abridged, two-volume version). New York: Dell Publishing, 1965.

Tubb, E.C. *The Winds of Gath.* Ace, 1982.
———. *Toyman.* Ace, 1982.
———. *Kalin.* Arrow: London, 1976.
———. *The Jester at Scar.* Ace, 1982.
———. *Lallia.* Ace, 1982.
———. *Jondelle.* Arrow: London, 1977.

Vance, Jack. *The Dying Earth.* 1950.
———. *Houses of Iszm.* 1954.
———. Lyonesse trilogy.
———. *Rhialto the Marvellous.* 1985.

Wells, H. G. *The Time Machine.* 1895.
———. *The War of the Worlds.* 1898.

Wilder, Laura Ingalls. *Little House in the Big Woods.* 1932.
———. *Little House on the Prairie.* 1935.
———. *Farmer Boy.* 1933.
———. *On the Banks of Plum Creek.* 1937.
———. *By the Shores of Silver Lake.* 1939.
———. *The Long Winter.* 1940.
———. *Little Town on the Prairie.* 1941.
———. *These Happy Golden Years.* 1943.
———. *The First Four Years.* 1968.
———. *On the Way Home.* 1962.
———. *West from Home.* 1974.

Wolfe, Gene. *The Book of the New Sun.* 1983.

Wong, Kar-Wai. *In the Mood for Love.* 2000.

Wylie, Philip. *The End of the Dream.* 1972.

PUBLISHING HISTORY

"Alas, Babylon and the Cuban Nukes," *New York Review of Science Fiction No. 340,* Dec 2016.

"Anglo-American Movies Responding to Hitler, 1936 to 1941" *New York Review of Science Fiction No. 314,* Oct 2014.

"Autopsy on SF," *New York Review of Science Fiction No. 110,* Oct 1997.

"Ballard's Debt to Hawthorne: 'Prima Belladonna,'" *New York Review of Science Fiction No. 316,* Dec 2014.

"Deciphering the Text Foundations of Traveller [sfrpg]," *The Internet Review of Science Fiction (Vol. II, No. 1),* Feb 2005.

"Languages of the Dying Sun," *Earth is But a Star* (edited by Damien Broderick, published by University of Western Australia Press), preprinted in *New York Review of Science Fiction No. 149,* Jan 2001.

"The Last Defender of Barsoom," *New York Review of Science Fiction No. 295,* Mar 2013.

"Little Proust on the Prairie," *New York Review of Science Fiction No. 129,* May 1999.

"Notes on 'The Prophets' Paradise' of *The King in Yellow*," *New York Review of Science Fiction No. 341,* Jun 2017.

"Notes for Survivors (1975)," *New York Review of Science Fiction No. 342*, Aug 2017.

"Raving on 'The Repairer of Reputations' by Robert W. Chambers," *New York Review of Science Fiction No. 317*, Jan 2015.

Review of Shane Carruth's features *Primer* (2004) and *Upstream Color* (2013) for *New York Review of Science Fiction No. 321*, May 2015.

"Science Fiction Rock (1969-1979): David Bowie and Gary Numan," *Internet Review of Science Fiction*, Jul 2008.

"SF Heresies #1 and #2," *New York Review of Science Fiction No. 183*, Nov 2003.

"SF Rock: The Human League," *New York Review of Science Fiction No. 315*, Nov 2014.

"Singularity and Toynbee" [unpublished]

"Some Informal Remarks on Michael Swanwick's *Stations of the Tide*," online 2000.

"Spike Jonez v. Sofia Coppola," *New York Review of Science Fiction No. 331*, Mar 2016.

"Toynbee and Science Fiction: Two Case Studies" [Asimov and de Camp], *New York Review of Science Fiction No. 250*, Jun 2009.

"Wes Anderson as a Great-Grandson of Edgar Rice Burroughs," *New York Review of Science Fiction No. 310*, Jun 2014.

BOOKS BY THIS AUTHOR

True Sf Anime

Can someone love anime while hating transforming mecha robots? Is there a world of Japanese animation beyond giant bubble-filled eyes and predictable plots?

This book of essays explores dozens of rare gems of anime, all built in the "true SF" tradition: movies and TV shows with real stories, real characters, and real explorations of the technological possibilities of the future. The works covered include Paprika, Planetes, Wings of Honneamise, The Melancholy of Haruhi Suzumiya, and more.

Roadside Picnic Revisited: Seven Articles On The Soviet Novel That Inspired The Film 'Stalker'

A collection of essays and a book review relating to "Roadside Picnic," the Soviet science fiction novel by Arkady and Boris Strugatsky. Topics include:

*Close reading of the novel to unlock its mysteries.
*Translation triumphs and errors.
*A British novel that had a profound influence on "Roadside Picnic."
*The critical reception of "Roadside Picnic" in the West.
*The original plan for "Roadside Picnic" and the terrible compromise that came.

Handbook Of Vance Space

A dictionary-style guide to the science fiction worlds of Jack Vance. A souvenir of the worlds you have visited in the past! A planning guide for your next excursion off world! A handy survival manual for unexpected occasions! A reference work on the science fiction of award-winning Grand Master Jack Vance! A handbook!

www.ingramcontent.com/pod-product-compliance
Lightning Source LLC
Chambersburg PA
CBHW031446040426
42444CB00007B/995